GREAT AUSSIE

★ ★ ★

JOKES BLOKES AND

Quotes

GREAT AUSSIE

★ ★ ★

JOKES ▸ BLOKES ◂ AND

Quotes

◆

Paul Taylor,

Henry Lawson, Steele Rudd, Edward Dyson,
A.B. 'Banjo' Paterson & W.T. Goodge

The Five Mile Press

The Five Mile Press Pty Ltd
1 Centre Road, Scoresby
Victoria 3179 Australia
www.fivemile.com.au

Part of the Bonnier Publishing Group
www.bonnierpublishing.com

First published in this collection 2013

Printed in Australia at Griffin Press.
Only wood grown from sustainable regrowth forests
is used in the manufacture of paper found in this book.

Icon illustrations copyright © Lottie Roue, 2013
Cover photo copyright © Melanie Faith Dove, 2013

Thanks to Tony Gerard for the laughs

National Library of Australia Cataloguing-in-Publication entry
Taylor, Paul.
Great aussie jokes, blokes and quotes / Paul Taylor, Henry
Lawson, Steele Rudd, Edward Dyson.
ISBN: 9781743465271 (pbk.)
Australian wit and humor
Lawson, Henry, 1867-1922
Rudd, Steele, 1868-1935
Dyson, Edward, 1865-1931
A824.3

• CONTENTS •

BLOKES

All Stories by Paul Taylor

QUOTES

STORIES

SLANG

GREAT AUSSIE

★ ★ ★

JOKES BLOKES AND

Quotes

• INTRODUCTION •

There is something for every Aussie male in this collection. Whether you are young, old or in-between, whether you were born here or arrived yesterday. The jokes are funny, the stories are classics, the blokes are heroes.

The short stories are from the nineteenth century when Australia's sense of national identity was just beginning to evolve. In fact the authors of these short stories, Henry Lawson, Steele Rudd and Edward Dyson, contributed to the emerging nation's sense of place, character and uniqueness.

These blokes wrote stories about living in the Australian bush, which is where all of us in this wonderful country still think we come from, even though most of us rarely go. If you really want a belly laugh, read Henry Lawson's *The Loaded Dog*.

The blokes are genuine heroes of sport, war, history and showbiz. From the genius general John Monash to the inimitable Barry Humphries, from brilliant Ricky Ponting to the king himself, Wally Lewis. And just how did we choose our heroes out of the many great Australians who exist? Well, they're awesome, and they just happen to be some of the many favourites of one our own favourite authors, Paul Taylor. He wrote all the profiles found in this collection.

But wait, there's more. A pithy collection of international quotes for every occasion. A choice assortment of true blue slang. Plus everything you need to know about Australian icons.

We really hope you enjoy this celebration of Australian life and language.

JOKES

• JOKES •

CONTENTS

DRINKING AND DRIVING
★ ★ ★

I would like to share an experience with you all – to do with drinking and driving.

As you know, some people have a brush with the authorities on their way home. Well I, for one, have done something about it.

The other night I was out for dinner and a few drinks. Having had far too much vino and, knowing full well that I was over the limit, I did something I have never done before – I took a bus home.

I arrived safely and without incident, which was a real surprise as I have never driven a bus before.

SILLY SIGNS
★ ★ ★

Sign over a gynaecologist's office
'Dr Jones, at your cervix.'

In a podiatrist's office
'Time wounds all heels.'

On a septic-tank truck
'Yesterday's meals-on-wheels'

•

At a proctologist's door
'To expedite your visit, please back in.'

•

On a plumber's truck
'We repair what your husband fixed.'

•

On another plumber's truck
'Dont sleep with a drip. Call your plumber.'

•

On a church's billboard
'Seven days without God makes one weak.'

•

At a towing company
'We don't charge an arm and a leg. We want tows.'

•

On an electrician's truck
'Let us remove your shorts.'

In a nonsmoking area
*'If we see smoke, we will assume you are on fire
and take appropriate action.'*

•

On a maternity room door
'Push. Push. Push.'

•

At an optometrist's office
*'If you don't see what you're looking for,
You've come to the right place.'*

•

On a taxidermist's window
'We really know our stuff.'

•

On a fence
'Salesmen welcome. Dog food is expensive!'

•

At a car dealership
'The best way to get back on your feet – miss a car payment.'

•

Outside a muffler shop
'No appointment necessary. We hear you coming.'

In a veterinarian's waiting room
'Be back in five minutes. Sit! Stay!'

•

In the front yard of a funeral home
'Drive carefully. We'll wait.'

•

At a propane filling station
'Thank heaven for little grills.'

•

Sign in a radiator shop
'Best place in town to take a leak.'

A NUN

A nun, badly needing to find a public toilet, walked into a local pub. The place was hopping with music and loud conversation and every once in a while the lights would turn off. Each time the lights would go out, the place would erupt into cheers. However, when the revellers saw the nun, the room went dead silent. She walked up to the bartender, and asked, *'May I please use the bathroom?'*

The bartender replied, *'OK, but I should warn you that there is a statue* of a naked man in there wearing only a fig leaf.'

'Well, in that case, I'll just look the other way', said the nun.

So the bartender showed the nun to the back of the pub. After a few minutes, she came back out, and the whole place stopped just long enough to give the nun a loud round of applause.

She went to the bartender and said, 'Sir, I don't understand. Why did they applaud for me just because I went to the bathroom?'

'Well, now they know you're one of us', said the bartender. 'Would you like a drink?'

'No, thank you, but I still don't understand,' said the puzzled nun.

'You see,' laughed the bartender, 'Every time someone lifts the fig leaf on that statue, the lights go out. Now, how about that drink?'

NEVER TOO LATE TO LEARN
★ ★ ★

An elderly man is stopped by the police around 2am and is asked where he is going at this time of night.

The man replies, 'I am on my way to a lecture about alcohol abuse and the effects it has on the human body, as well as smoking and staying out late.'

The officer then asks, 'Really? Who is giving that lecture at this time of night?'

The man replies, 'That would be my wife.'

COSTA CONCORDIA
★ ★ ★

How do they serve alcoholic drinks
on Italian cruise ships?
On the rocks

•

What vegetables do you get with
dinner on Italian cruise ships?
Leeks

•

What's the fastest way to get off an Italian cruise ship?
Follow the captain

•

When the captain of the *Costa Concordia*
was asked if he knew where
he was going he replied
'Off course'

•

So the captain of the *Costa Concordia*
will soon be in the dock.
That's more than can be said for his ship.

The *Costa Concordia* is probably
the most expensive thing to go down
in Italy since Berlusconi's last hooker.

•

What's the difference between the Italian economy
and the *Costa Concordia*?
Nothing. The bottom's dropped out of both.

A TOURIST

A tourist in Vienna is going through a graveyard when all of a sudden he hears music. No one is around, so he starts searching for the source. He finally locates the origin and finds it is coming from a grave with a headstone that reads '*Ludwig van Beethoven, 1770–1827*'. Then he realises that the music is the 9th Symphony and it is being played backwards!

Puzzled, he leaves the graveyard and persuades a friend to return with him. By the time they arrive back at the grave, the music has changed. This time it is the 7th Symphony, but like the previous piece, it is being played backwards.

Curious, the men agree to consult a music scholar. When they return with the expert, the 5th Symphony is playing, again backwards.

The expert notices that the symphonies are being played in the reverse order in which they were composed, the 9th, then the 7th, then the 5th.

By the next day the word has spread and a crowd has gathered around the grave. They are all listening to the 2nd Symphony being played backwards. Just then the graveyard's caretaker ambles up to the group.

Someone in the group asks him if he has an explanation for the music.

'I would have thought it was obvious,' the caretaker says.

'He's decomposing.'

UNCLE DEREK

Rrriiiiinnnnggg, rrriiiiinnnngg.

'Hello?'

'Hi sweetie. This is Daddy. Is Mummy near the phone?'

'No, Daddy. She's upstairs in the bedroom with Uncle Derek.'

After a brief pause, Daddy says, *'But sweetie, you haven't got an Uncle Derek.'*

'Oh yes I do, and he's upstairs in the room with Mummy, Right now.'

Brief pause

Uh, okay then, this is what I want you to do. Put the phone down on the table, run upstairs. Knock on the bedroom door and shout to Mummy that Daddy's car just pulled into the driveway.'

'Okay, Daddy, just a minute.'

A few minutes later the little girl comes back to the phone. *'I did it, Daddy.'*

'And what happened, honey?'

'Well, Mummy got all scared, jumped out of bed with no clothes on and ran around screaming. Then she tripped over the rug, hit her head on the dresser. And now she isn't moving at all!'

'Oh my God!!! What about your Uncle Derek?'

'He jumped out of the bed with no clothes on, too... He was all scared and he jumped out of the back window. And into the swimming pool... But I guess he didn't know that you took out the water last week to clean it. He hit the bottom of the pool and I think he's dead.'

Long pause

Longer pause

Even longer pause

Then Daddy says, *'Swimming pool? Is this 9486-5731?'*

'No, I think you have the wrong number...'

THE WIFE'S NICKNAME

★ ★ ★

I was listening to the radio this morning when the host invited callers to reveal the nicknames they had for their wives: Best call was from the brave chap who called his wife *'Harvey Norman'* – explaining ... *'Absolutely no interest for 36 months'*

JOEY PAGANO

★ ★ ★

'Bless me Father, for I have sinned. I have been with a loose girl.'

The priest asks, *'Is that you, little Joey Pagano?'*

'Yes, Father, it is.'

'And who was the girl you were with?'

'I can't tell you, Father. I don't want to ruin her reputation.'

'Well, Joey, I'm sure to find out her name sooner or later, so you may as well tell me now. Was it Tina Minetti?'

'I cannot say.'

'Was it Teresa Mazzarelli?'

'I'll never tell.'

'Was it Nina Capelli?'

'I'm sorry, but I cannot name her.'

'Was it Cathy Piriano?'

'My lips are sealed.'

'Was it Rosa DiAngelo, then?'

'Please, Father, I cannot tell you.'

The priest sighs in frustration... *'You're very tight lipped, and I admire that. But you've sinned and have to atone. You cannot be an altar boy now for four months. Now you go and behave yourself.'*

Joey walks back to his pew, and his friend Franco slides over and whispers, *'What'd you get?'*

'Four months vacation and five good leads.'

THE IRISH MILLIONAIRE

Mick, from Dublin, appeared on *Who Wants To Be A Millionaire* and towards the end of the program had already won 500,000 euros.

'You've done very well so far,' said the show's presenter, *'but for a million euros you've only got one life-line left, phone a friend. Everything is riding on this question. Will you go for it?'*

'Sure.' said Mick. *'I'll have a go!'*

'Which of the following birds does not build its own nest?

a) Sparrow
b) Thrush
c) Magpie
d) Cuckoo?'

'I haven't got a clue.' said Mick, 'So I'll use my last lifeline and phone my friend Paddy back home in Dublin ...'

Mick called up his mate, and told him the circumstances and repeated the question to him.

'Bloody hell, Mick!' cried Paddy. 'Dat's simple, it's a cuckoo.'

'Are you sure?'

'I'm bloody sure.'

Mick hung up the phone and told the presenter,

'I'll go with cuckoo as my answer.'

'Is that your final answer?' asked the presenter.

'Dat it is.'

There was a long, long pause and then the presenter screamed, 'Cuckoo is the correct answer! Mick, you've won one million euros!'

The next night, Mick invited Paddy to their local pub to buy him a drink.

'Tell me, Paddy? How in Heaven's name did you know it was da cuckoo that doesn't build its own nest?'

'Because he lives in a fookin clock!'

WHAT IS CELIBACY?

Celibacy can be a choice in life, or a condition imposed by circumstances.

While attending a marriage retreat, my wife and I listened to the instructor declare, *'It is essential that husbands and wives know the things that are important to each other.'*

He then addressed the men, *'Can you name and describe your wife's favourite flower?'*

I leaned over, touched my wife's hand gently, and whispered, *'Self-raising flour, isn't it?'*

And thus began my life of celibacy...

CHRISTMAS THOUGHTFULNESS

A couple was Christmas shopping on Christmas Eve and the whole place was heaving, packed with other last-minute shoppers.

Walking through the shopping centre the surprised wife looked up from a window display and noticed her husband was nowhere to be seen. She knew they had lots still to do and she became very upset. She rummaged in her handbag and found her mobile phone then used it to call her husband to ask him where he was.

The husband in a calm voice replied *'Darling, you remember the jewellery shop we went into five years ago, where you fell in love with that diamond necklace that we could not afford and I told you that one day I would get it for you...?'*

His wife's eyes filled with tears of emotion, she began to cry softly and stifling a sob she whispered *'Yes, I remember that jewellery shop...'*

'Well,' he said, *'I'm in the pub next to it!'*

HOW TO HANDLE A HUSBAND

—— ★ ★ ★ ——

A couple was celebrating their golden wedding anniversary on the beaches in Montego Bay, Jamaica.

Their domestic tranquillity had long been the talk of the town. People would say, *'What a peaceful and loving couple.'*

The local newspaper reporter was inquiring as to the secret of their long and happy marriage.

The husband replied, *'Well, it dates back to our honeymoon in America. We visited the Grand Canyon, in Arizona, and took a trip down to the bottom of the canyon, by horse. We hadn't gone too far when my wife's horse stumbled and she almost fell off.*

'We proceeded a little further and her horse stumbled again. Again my wife quietly said, "That's twice."

'We hadn't gone a half-mile when the horse stumbled for the third time my wife quietly removed a revolver from her purse and shot the horse dead.

'I shouted at her, "What's wrong with you, Woman! Why did you shoot the poor animal like that, are you *%&#@$ crazy!?"

'She looked at me, and quietly said, "That's once."

'And from that moment we have lived happily ever after.'

FIVE MINUTE MANAGEMENT COURSE

★ ★ ★

> LESSON 1 <

A man is getting into the shower just as his wife is finishing up her shower, when the doorbell rings. The wife quickly wraps herself in a towel and runs downstairs. When she opens the door, there stands Bob, the next-door neighbour.

Before she says a word, Bob says, *'I'll give you $800 to drop that towel.'*

After thinking for a moment, the woman drops her towel and stands naked in front of Bob.

After a few seconds, Bob hands her $800 and leaves.

The woman wraps back up in the towel and goes back upstairs.

When she gets to the bathroom, her husband asks, *'Who was that?'*

'It was Bob the next door neighbour,' she replies.

'Great!' the husband says, *'did he say anything about the $800 he owes me?'*

MORAL OF THE STORY

If you share critical information pertaining to credit and risk with your shareholders in time, you may be in a position to prevent avoidable exposure.

A priest offered a nun a lift. She got in and crossed her legs, forcing her gown to reveal a leg. The priest nearly had an accident. After controlling the car, he stealthily slid his hand up her leg.

The nun said, *'Father, remember Psalm 129?'*

The priest removed his hand. But, changing gears, he let his hand slide up her leg again. The nun once again said, *'Father, remember Psalm 129?'*

The priest apologised *'Sorry sister but the flesh is weak.'*

Arriving at the convent, the nun sighed heavily and went on her way.

On his arrival at the church, the priest rushed to look up Psalm 129. It said, *'Go forth and seek, further up, you will find glory.'*

MORAL OF THE STORY

If you are not well informed in your job, opportunities for advancement will pass right by you.

> LESSON 3 <

A sales rep, an administration clerk and the manager are walking to lunch when they find an antique oil lamp. They rub it and a genie comes out.

The genie says, *'I'll give each of you just one wish.'*

'Me first! Me first!' says the admin clerk. *'I want to be on the open sea, driving a speedboat, without a care in the world.'* Puff! She's gone.

'*Me next! Me next!*' says the sales rep. '*I want to be on Hamilton Island, relaxing on the beach with my personal masseuse, an endless supply of Pina Coladas and the love of my life.*' Puff! He's gone.

'*OK, you're up,*' the genie says to the manager.

The manager says, '*I want those two back in the office after lunch.*'

MORAL OF THE STORY

Always let your boss have the first say.

An eagle was sitting on a tree resting, doing nothing. A small rabbit saw the eagle and asked him, '*Can I also sit like you and do nothing?*'

The eagle answered, '*Sure, why not.*'

So, the rabbit sat on the ground below the eagle and rested. All of a sudden, a fox appeared, jumped on the rabbit and ate it.

MORAL OF THE STORY

To be sitting and doing nothing, you must be sitting very, very high up.

A turkey was chatting with a bull.

'*I would love to be able to get to the top of that tree,*' sighed the turkey, '*but I haven't got the energy.*'

'Well, why don't you nibble on some of my droppings?' replied the bull. 'They're packed with nutrients.'

The turkey pecked at a lump of dung, and found it actually gave him enough strength to reach the lowest branch of the tree.

The next day, after eating some more dung, he reached the second branch. Finally after a fourth night, the turkey was proudly perched at the top of the tree.

He was promptly spotted by a farmer, who shot him out of the tree.

MORAL OF THE STORY

Bullshit might get you to the top, but it won't keep you there.

> LESSON 6 <

A little bird was flying south for the winter. It was so cold the bird froze and fell to the ground into a large field. While he was lying there, a cow came by and shat on him.

As the frozen bird lay there in the pile of cow dung, he began to realise how warm he was. The dung was actually thawing him out! He lay there all warm and happy, and soon began to sing for joy.

A passing cat heard the bird singing and came to investigate. Following the sound, the cat discovered the bird under the pile of cow dung, and promptly dug him out and ate him.

MORAL OF THE STORY

Not everyone who shits on you is your enemy. Not everyone who gets you out of shit is your friend. And when you're in deep shit, it's best to keep your mouth shut!

This concludes the five minute management course.

THE UNDERTAKER'S BLACK EYE

Roy, an undertaker, recently came home with a black eye.

'*What happened to you?*' asked his wife.

'*I had a terrible day,*' replied Roy. '*I had to go to a hotel and pick up a man who had died in his sleep. When I got there, the manager said they couldn't get him into a body bag because he had this huge erection. Anyway, I went up and sure enough there was this big naked guy lying on the bed with this huge erection. So I grabbed it with both hands and tried to snap it in half.*'

'*I see,*' said his wife, '*but how did you get the black eye?*'

Roy replied '*Wrong room.*'

THE PIRATE IN THE BAR

★ ★ ★

A pirate walked into a bar, and the bartender said, *'Hey, I haven't seen you in a while. What happened? You look terrible.'*

What do you mean?' said the pirate, *'I feel fine.'*

'What about the wooden leg? You didn't have that before.'

'Well,' said the pirate, *'We were in a battle, and I got hit with a cannon ball, but I'm fine now.'*

The bartender replied, *'Well, OK, but what about that hook? What happened to your hand?'*

The pirate explained, *'We were in another battle. I boarded a ship and got into a sword fight. My hand was cut off. I got fitted with a hook but I'm fine, really.'*

'What about that eye patch?'

'Oh,' said the pirate, *'One day we were at sea, and a flock of birds flew over. I looked up, and one of them shat in my eye.'*

'You're kidding,' said the bartender. *'You couldn't lose an eye just from bird shit.'*

'It was my first day with the hook.'

THE PENGUIN
★ ★ ★

Did you ever wonder why there are no dead penguins on the ice in Antarctica – where do they go?

It is a known fact that the penguin is a very ritualistic bird which lives an extremely ordered and complex life. The 2005 French movie *The March of the Penguins* documented some of their habits.

The penguin is very committed to its family and will mate for life, as well as maintaining a form of compassionate contact with its offspring throughout its life.

If a penguin is found dead on the ice surface, other members of the family and social circle have been known to dig holes in the ice, using their vestigial wings and beaks, until the hole is deep enough for the dead bird to be rolled into and buried.

The male penguins then gather in a circle around the fresh grave and sing.

'Freeze a jolly good fellow, Freeze a jolly good fellow.'

'Then they kick him in the icehole.'

You really didn't believe that I know anything about penguins, did you?

TWO HILLBILLIES
★ ★ ★

Two hillbillies walk into a restaurant. While having a bite to eat, they talk about their moonshine operation.

Suddenly, a woman at a nearby table, who is eating a sandwich, begins to cough. After a minute or so, it becomes apparent that she is in real distress.

One of the hillbillies looks at her and says, *'Kin ya swallar?'*

The woman shakes her head no.

Then he asks, *'Kin ya breathe?'*

The woman begins to turn blue and shakes her head no.

The hillbilly walks over to the woman, lifts up her dress, yanks down her drawers and quickly gives her right butt cheek a lick with his tongue.

The woman is so shocked that she has a violent spasm and the obstruction flies out of her mouth. As she begins to breathe again, the hillbilly walks slowly back to his table.

His partner says, *'Ya know, I'd heerd of that there "Hind Lick Maneuver" but I ain't niver seed nobody do it!'*

THE YOUNG COUPLE
— ★ ★ ★ —

A young couple joined a new church and the pastor told them,

'We require all new member couples to abstain from sex for one whole month.'

The couple agreed, but after two weeks returned to see the pastor. The wife was crying and the husband was obviously depressed.

'You are back so soon, is there a problem?' inquired the pastor.

'We did not manage to abstain from sex for the required month,' the young man replied sadly. *'The first week we managed to abstain through sheer willpower. The second week was terrible and as we began the third week we were powerless.'*

The pastor asked what happened.

The young man replied, *'My wife reached for a can of paint and dropped it. When she bent over to pick it up, I was overcome with lust and I had my way with her right then and there. It was lustful, loud, and passionate. It lasted over an hour and when we were done we were both drenched in sweat.'*

The pastor lowered his head and said sternly, *'You understand this means you will not be welcome in our church.'*

'We understand,' said the young man, hanging his head, *'We're not welcome at the hardware shop either.'*

ID TEN T ERROR

— ★ ★ ★ —

I was having trouble with my computer.

So I called Eric, the 11-year-old next door, whose bedroom looks like Mission Control and asked him to come over. Eric clicked a couple of buttons and solved the problem.

As he was walking away, I called after him, *'So, what was wrong?'*

He replied, *'It was an ID ten T error.'*

I didn't want to appear stupid, but nonetheless inquired, *'An, ID ten T error? What's that? In case I need to fix it again.'*

Eric grinned... *'Haven't you ever heard of an ID ten T error before?'*

'No,' I replied.

'Write it down,' he said, *'and I think you'll figure it out.'*

So I wrote it down - I D 1 0 T

I used to like Eric, the little bastard.

IT SUCKS TO GET OLD

— ★ ★ ★ —

An 85-year-old man was requested by his doctor for a sperm count as part of his physical examination

The doctor gave the man a jar and said, *'Take this jar home and bring back a semen sample tomorrow.'*

The next day the 85-year-old man reappeared at the doctor's office and gave him the jar, which was as clean and empty as on the previous day.

The doctor asked what happened and the man explained *'Well, doc, it's like this – first I tried with my right hand, but nothing. Then I tried with my left hand, but still nothing... Then I asked my wife for help. She tried with her right hand, then with her left, still nothing... She tried with her mouth, first with the teeth in, then with her teeth out, still nothing. We even called up Arleen, the lady next door and she tried too, first with both hands, then an armpit, and she even tried squeezing' it between her knees, but still nothing.'*

The doctor was shocked. *'You asked your neighbour?'*

The old man replied, *'Yep. None of us could get the jar open!'*

I know what you were thinking! Shame on you.

LONESOME COWBOY

An old cowboy sat down at the bar and ordered a drink.

As he sat sipping his drink, a young woman sat down next to him.

She turned to the cowboy and asked, *'Are you a real cowboy?'*

He replied, *'Well, I've spent my whole life breaking colts, working cows, going to rodeos, fixing fences, pulling calves, bailing hay, doctoring calves, cleaning my barn, fixing flats, working on tractors, and feeding my dogs, so I guess I am a cowboy.'*

She said, *'I'm a lesbian. I spend my whole day thinking about naked women. As soon as I get up in the morning, I think about naked women. When I shower, I think about naked women. When I watch TV, I think about naked women. It seems everything makes me think of naked women.'*

The two sat sipping in silence.

A little while later, a man sat down on the other side of the old cowboy and asked, *'Are you a real cowboy?'*

He replied, *'I always thought I was, but I just found out I'm a lesbian.'*

TALKING DOG FOR SALE

★ ★ ★

A man sees a sign outside a house *'Talking Dog For Sale.'* He rings the bell, the owner appears and tells him the dog can be viewed in the back garden.

The man sees a very nice looking Labrador retriever sitting there.

'Do you really talk?' he asks the dog.

'Yes,' the Labrador replies.

After recovering from the shock of hearing the dog talk, the man asks, *'So, tell me your story.'*

The Labrador looks up and says, *'Well, I discovered that I could talk when I was pretty young. I wanted to help my country, so I contacted the government. In no time at all they had me jetting from country to country, sitting in rooms with spies and world leaders because no one imagined that a dog would be eavesdropping. I was one of their most valuable spies for eight years. But the jetting around really tired me out, and I knew I wasn't getting any younger so I decided to settle down. I signed up for a job at the airport to do some undercover security work, wandering near suspicious characters and listening in. I uncovered some incredible dealings and was awarded several medals. I got married, had a few puppies, and now I've just retired.'*

The man is amazed. He goes back into the house and asks the owner how much he wants for the dog.

'Ten dollars,' the owner says.

'But this dog is absolutely amazing! Why on earth are you selling him so cheaply?'

'Because he's a lying bastard, he's never been out of the garden.'

THE TEENAGER

I took my dad to the mall the other day to buy some new shoes (he is 76). We decided to grab a bite at the food court.

I noticed he was watching a teenager sitting next to him. The teenager had spiked hair in all different colours – green, red, orange and blue.

My dad kept staring at her. The teenager kept looking, finding my dad staring every time.

When the teenager had had enough, she sarcastically asked, *'What's the matter old man, never done anything wild in your life?'*

Knowing my dad, I quickly swallowed my food so that I would not choke on his response; I knew he would have a good one!

In classic style he responded without batting an eyelid.

'Got stoned once and had sex with a parrot. I was just wondering if you might be my kid.'

AN IRISH DAUGHTER

An Irish daughter had not been home for over five years. Upon her return, her father cursed her heavily.

'Where have ye been all this time, child? Why did ye not write to us, not even a line? Why didn't ye call? Can ye not understand what ye put yer old Mother thru?'

The girl, crying, replied, *'Sniff, sniff... Dad... I became a prostitute.'*

'Ye what!? Get out a here, ye shameless harlot! Sinner! You're a disgrace to this Catholic family.'

'OK, Dad... as ye wish. I only came back to give mum this luxurious fur coat, title deed to a ten-bedroom mansion, plus a five million dollar savings certificate. For me little brother, this gold Rolex. And for ye Daddy, the sparkling new Mercedes limited edition convertible that's parked outside plus a membership to the country club...(takes a breath)...and an invitation for ye all to spend New Year's Eve on board my new yacht in the Riviera.'

'What was it ye said ye had become?' says Dad.

Girl, crying again, *'A prostitute, Daddy! Sniff, sniff.'*

'Oh! Be Jesus! Ye scared me half to death, girl! I thought ye said a Protestant! Come here and give yer old Dad a hug!'

PADDY AND MICK

★ ★ ★

Paddy and Mick were walking along a street in London. Paddy looked in one of the shop windows and saw a sign that caught his eye. The sign read: Suits £5.00 each, Shirts £2.00 each, Trousers £2.50 per pair.

Paddy said to his pal, *'Mick look at the prices! We could buy a whole lot of dose and when we get back to Ireland we could make a fortune. Now when we go in you stay quiet, okay? Let me do all da talking 'cause if they hear our accents, they might think we're thickos from Ireland and try to screw us. I'll put on my best English accent.'*

'Roight y'are Paddy, I'll keep me mouth shut, so I will. You do all da business,' said Mick.

They go in and Paddy said in a posh voice, *'Hello, my good man. I'll take 50 suits at £5.00 each, 100 shirts at £2.00 each, and 50 pairs of trousers at £2.50 each. I'll back up me truck ready to load 'em on, so I will.'*

The owner of the shop said quietly, *'You're from Ireland, aren't you?'*

'Well, yes,' said a surprised Paddy. *'What gave it away?'*

The owner replied *'This is a dry-cleaners.'*

★ ★ ★

Five rules for men to follow for a happy life.

RULE 1

It's important to have a woman who helps at home, cooks from time to time, cleans up and has a job.

RULE 2

It's important to have a woman who can make you laugh.

RULE 3

It's important to have a woman who you can trust and who doesn't lie to you.

RULE 4

It's important to have a woman who is good in bed and who likes to be with you.

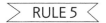

> RULE 5 <

It's very, very important that these four woman do not know each other or you could end up dead like me.

PARKINSONS OR ALZHEIMERS?

An old woman was asked, *'At your ripe age, what would you prefer to get – Parkinsons or Alzheimers?'*

The wise one answered, *'Definitely Parkinsons. Better to spill half my wine than to forget where I keep the bottle..!'*

MEDICARE

The phone rings and the lady of the house answers, *'Hello.'*

'Mrs Sanders, please.'

'Speaking.'

'Mrs Sanders, this is Doctor Jones at Saint Agnes Laboratory. When your husband's doctor sent his biopsy to the lab last week, a biopsy from another Mr Sanders arrived as well. We are now uncertain which one belongs to your

husband. Frankly, either way the results are not too good.'

'What do you mean?' Mrs Sanders asks nervously.

'Well, one of the specimens tested positive for Alzheimer's and the other one tested positive for HIV. We can't tell which is which.'

'That's dreadful! Can you do the test again?' questioned Mrs Sanders.

'Normally we can, but Medicare only pay for these expensive tests once.'

'Well, what am I supposed to do now?'

'We recommend that you drop your husband off somewhere in the middle of town. If he finds his way home, don't sleep with him.'

MY JOB SEARCH
★ ★ ★

My first job was working in an orange juice factory,
but I got canned. Couldn't concentrate.

•

Then I worked in the woods as a lumberjack,
but just couldn't hack it, so they gave me the axe.

•

After that, I tried being a tailor, but wasn't suited for it
mainly because as a job, it was just sew-sew.

Next, I tried working in a muffler factory,
but that was too exhausting.

•

Then, tried being a chef – figured it would add a little spice to
my life, but just didn't have the thyme.

•

Next, I attempted being a deli worker, but any way I sliced it...
Couldn't cut the mustard.

•

My best job was a musician, but eventually
found I wasn't noteworthy.

•

I studied a long time to become a doctor,
but didn't have any patience.

•

Next, was a job in a shoe factory...
Tried hard but just didn't fit in.

•

I became a professional fisherman,
but discovered I couldn't live on my net income.

•

Managed to get a good job working for a pool maintenance
company, but the work was just too draining.

So then I got a job in a gym,
but they said I wasn't fit for the job.

•

After many years of trying to find steady work,
I finally got a job as a historian –
until I realised there was no future in it.

•

My last job was working in a coffee shop,
But had to quit because it was the same old grind.

•

So, I tried retirement and found
I'm perfect for the job!

WHEN I SAY I'M BROKE, I'M BROKE

★ ★ ★

A little old lady answered a knock on the door one day, to be confronted by a well-dressed young man carrying a vacuum cleaner. *'Good morning,'* said the young man. *'If I could take a couple minutes of your time, I would like to demonstrate the very latest in high-powered vacuum cleaners.'*

'Go away!' said the old lady. *'I'm broke and haven't got any money!'* and she proceeded to close the door.

Quick as a flash, the young man wedged his foot in the door and pushed it wide open. *'Don't be too hasty!'* he said. *'Not until you have at least seen my demonstration.'*

And with that, he emptied a bucket of horse manure onto her hallway carpet. *'Now if this vacuum cleaner does not remove all traces of this horse manure from your carpet, Madam, I will personally eat the remainder.'*

The old lady stepped back and said, *'Well, let me get you a fork, because they cut off my electricity this morning.'*

FATHER O'MALLEY

Father O'Malley rose from his bed one morning.

It was a fine spring day in his new parish.

He walked to the window of his bedroom to get a deep breath of the beautiful day outside. He then noticed there was a donkey lying dead in the middle of his front lawn. He promptly called the local police station.

The conversation went like this:

'Good morning. This is Sergeant Jones. How might I help you?'

'And the best of the day te yerself. This is Father O'Malley at St Ann's Catholic Church. There's a donkey lying dead in me front lawn and would ye be so kind as to send a couple o'yer lads to take care of the matter?'

Sergeant Jones, considering himself to be quite a wit and recognising the Irish accent, thought he would have a little fun with the good father, replied, *'Well now Father, it was always my impression that you people took care of the last rites!'*

There was dead silence on the line for a moment . . .

Father O'Malley then replied *'Aye,' 'tis certainly true; but we are also obliged to notify the next of kin first, which is the reason for me call.'*

QUESTIONS YOU JUST CAN'T ANSWER
★ ★ ★

Why doesn't Tarzan have a beard when
he lives in the jungle without a razor?

•

Why do we press harder on a remote control when
we know the batteries are flat?

•

Why do banks charge a fee on 'insufficient funds'
when they know there is not enough?

•

Why do kamikaze pilots wear helmets?

•

Why does someone believe you when you say
there are four billion stars,
but check when you say the paint is wet?

Whose idea was it to put an 's' in the word 'lisp'?

•

What is the speed of darkness?

•

Why is it that people say they 'slept like a baby'
when babies wake up every two hours?

•

If the temperature is zero outside today and it's going to be
twice as cold tomorrow, how cold will it be?

•

Do married people live longer than single ones
or does it only seem longer?

•

How is it that we put man on the moon before we figured out
it would be a good idea to put wheels on luggage?

•

Why do people pay to go up tall buildings and then put money
in binoculars to look at things on the ground?

•

Did you ever stop and wonder who was the first
person to look at a cow and say,
*'I think I'll squeeze these pink dangly things here,
and drink whatever comes out?'*

Who was the first person to say, *'See that chicken there...*
I'm gonna eat the next thing that comes outta it's bum.'?

•

Why do toasters always have a setting so high
that could burn the toast to a horrible crisp,
which no decent human being would eat?

•

Why is there a light in the fridge and not in the freezer?

•

Why do people point to their wrist when asking for the time,
but don't point to their bum
when they ask where the bathroom is?

•

Why does your gynaecologist leave the room when you get
undressed if they are going to look up there anyway?

•

Why does Goofy stand erect while
Pluto remains on all fours? They're both dogs!

•

If quizzes are quizzical, what are tests?

•

If corn oil is made from corn, and vegetable oil is made from
vegetables, then what is baby oil made from?

• ICONS •

> VEGEMITE <

In 1923 a Melbourne salesman, Fred Walker, won a contract with Carlton and United Breweries to provide them with the necessary yeast for their beer production. The enterprising and resourceful Walker immediately hired a chemist named Callister to develop a yeast extract by-product, which we know today as Vegemite.

Once the product had been made to Walker's satisfaction, Walker ran a competition to find a name for it. He presented his daughter Sheila with a list of proposed names sent in by the public. She favoured Vegemite, and the name was chosen.

Five years later the closest spread in flavour to Vegemite, the English beef extract, Marmite, was yeilding greater sales than Vegemite. Fred Walker promptly changed the name Vegemite to Parwill, with the acompanying slogan, *'If Marmite, Parwill!'* But the consumers were not enthusiastic, and the Vegemite name quickly resurfaced. In 1926 The Fred Walker company became known as Kraft Walker Cheese Company, and is presently an American-owned company.

The Vegemite recipe contains a blend of yeasts as well as celery extract, onion extract and salt, but the exact breakdown of ingredients remains a closely guarded secret. The unusual dark spread is loved by Australians and it is likely to remain a uniquely Australian icon for years to come.

• ICONS •

Although at first glance the rising sun badge looks like just that –
a rising sun – it is in fact a representation of a brace of bayonets.

Major Joseph Gordon was commander of Fort Glenvill, a post
designed to protect Adelaide from sea invasion. Commander William
Cresswell, Commandant of the Naval Forces of South Australia,
created a trophy (referred to as the rising sun) to symbolise defence
and Major Gordon took this trophy with him on lecture tours.

In 1899 Gordon met up with an old acquaintance, Hutton, in South
Africa, and gave Hutton the trophy as a gift. They had previously met
years earlier in New South Wales where Hutton was involved in the
military.

Hutton was soon after appointed the Commander in Chief
of Australian forces and had the task of designing a badge for the
Australian forces in South Africa, to distinguish them from the British
troops.

Hutton was not willing to consider designs featuring Australian
plants or animals, for he sought a martial, rather than an Australiana,
look. His attention turned to the bayonet trophy of arms which hung
on the wall over his office door in the Victoria Barracks. He proposed
that this should be the basis of the badge's design. Over the years the
design has varied only marginally, and it continues to be seen by most
as a rising sun, rather than a trophy of bayonets.

Having many places of rest throughout its history, the original rising
sun trophy now sits in public view at the main entrance to Russell Hill
Defence Headquarters in Canberra.

• BLOKES •

CONTENTS

• JOHN SIMPSON •

THE STRETCHER BEARER SAINT

Just before dawn, at about 5am, on Sunday 25 April 1915, C Section, 1st Australian Division, Australian Imperial Force rowed ashore from the transport boat *Devanha* and the men leapt from the boat and waded ashore at Gallipoli. The first into the water was killed immediately. Private John Simpson was the second man in the water. The third man died beside him. Of the 1500 men in the first wave, 755 remained in active service at the end of the day. The rest – half of the landing force – were killed or wounded.

By dawn on the second day, the Turkish troops on the high ground looked down their gun barrels at the Australians, pinned to 200 hectares, threatened from almost every angle except the sea at their backs. Working all day, under constant fire, Simpson carried the wounded, slipping and sliding down the steep slopes to the beach at Anzac Cove. Stretcher bearing was exhausting, agonising and dangerous work. Then, late on that day, Simpson, struggling under the weight of a heavy, wounded digger, saw a donkey grazing in a hollow, oblivious to the battle. Bullets buzzed around him, but Simpson made a head stall and lead from bandages and field dressings and lifted the wounded man onto the donkey he later named 'Murphy'.

From then, Simpson and the donkey were a team. From around 6.30am, they would go to and fro the two kilometres up Shrapnel Gully, the main supply route to the front line, into Monash Valley and onto the deadly zone around Quinn's Post, where the opposing trenches were just 20 metres apart. To the left of Quinn's Post was Dead Man's Ridge, held by the Turks and from where they were able to snipe right down Shrapnel Gully. Through this sniper fire and shrapnel Simpson would bring water for the wounded. He would leave Murphy under cover while he tended the casualties and then carry them to the donkey.

Then they'd go back – a dozen or more times a day and into the night often continuing until as late as 3am. He made the two-kilometre trip through sniper fire and shrapnel, and dismissed all warnings of the certain death he faced with the reply, *'My troubles'* – an early version of the classic Australian expression, *'She'll be right, mate.'* The diggers loved and revered him.

Simpson lasted just 25 days. On the morning of 19 May he and Murphy went out again. It was before breakfast. *'Never mind,'* he called out. *'Get me a good dinner when I come back.'* He didn't come back. Simpson was bringing two wounded men along a creek bed when a Turkish sniper shot him through the heart.

• JOHN MONASH •

Sir John Monash and Dame Nellie Melba are each commemorated on one side of the Australian $100 note. In the 1920s they were accepted as the greatest living Australians. Today Monash's name is known to most Australians, but only as the name of a freeway and a university. Melba, who was an international superstar, is today remembered as the name of a peach dessert and a piece of toast.

Both deserve to be remembered and respected by all Australians.

In May 1918 the Australian Imperial Force, after years of fighting under the overall command of British generals in the First World War, were given wonderful news. Lieutenant-General Sir John Monash was to be their senior commander. Monash was one of them, an Australian. And the diggers believed that Monash, who had been with them from the landing at Gallipoli, was the man most likely to lead them to victory – and to get them out with the least possible casualties. They had a saying that Monash *would command a division better than a brigade and a corps better than a division*.

Monash, they knew, did not believe that men should be sent on heroic but senseless frontal attacks in which they would inevitably be cut down. Instead they should advance with the protection of tanks, mortars and aeroplanes.

The Australian Corps that Monash was in command of numbered 166,000 men.

Three weeks later Monash showed why the diggers cheered the news of his promotion. Monash was given the task of planning the Battle of Hamel.

His battle plan was innovative, little short of revolutionary, in its use of aviation, artillery and armour. Using 7000 Australian troops and some Americans newly arrived in France, Monash plotted an amazingly brief 90-minute battle. It took three minutes longer than he had calculated. At the end of the Battle of Hamel the Allied High Command, after years of fighting with very little to show for it other than the deaths of hundreds of thousands of men, was astonished. This was a radically different way to win. At Hamel the Australians under Monash showed that the tide could be turned, the war could be won, and won in the way of the victory at Hamel.

John Monash was born in West Melbourne on 27 June 1865. His father had migrated there from Poland during the gold rush, changed his name to Monash and opened a general store at Jerilderie. John went to the public school there from 1875 to 1877, during the time that Ned Kelly held up the town and, it's said, invited young John Monash to hold the reins of his horse for him.

Back in Melbourne, John, a precocious and intelligent boy, was equal top of his school, Scotch College, and won the highest marks in mathematics in the state. But for all his brilliance Monash led a turbulent private life. He graduated from Melbourne University as a civil engineer, but in the depths of the depression of 1890s he lost his job. He had got a law degree by last-minute cramming, and for a while he and a partner were in demand in cases involving civil engineering. Then they concentrated on bridge building and were doing well until they ran into financial difficulties and, deeply in debt, broke up.

Monash repaid his debts and by 1905 was making his mark in business, with a concrete company, and in the social life of Melbourne. He had become involved in the military, gaining a commission with the North Melbourne Battery of the Garrison Artillery, whose fixed guns defended the Victorian ports. And when the First World War broke out in 1914, Monash was briefly chosen to be chief censor before being appointed to the command of the 4th Infantry Brigade and landing with the brigade at Gallipoli on the evening of 24 April 1915.

Monash survived the murderous welcome waiting for them and by surviving saved the lives of untold numbers of men in the great battles to come.

• DOUGLAS MAWSON •

>   THE GREAT ESCAPE   <

In 1911 an Australian geologist, Douglas Mawson, led an expedition to Antarctica to set up base at Commonwealth Bay, a dark, featureless landscape where the wind can reach 300 kilometres an hour. On this dark stage Mawson was to perform one of the great tales of courage and endurance – a story that, strangely, has never been as celebrated as it deserves.

It began mundanely enough on 14 December 1912. Mawson, a Swiss mountaineer named Dr Xavier Mertz and Lieutenant Ninnis of the Royal Fusiliers were making good progress on a scientific expedition across the ice when Mertz, on skis and breaking a trail for the sledges, stopped at a bridged crevasse the party had to cross.

He and Mawson gauged the danger and ran quickly across the chasm.

They looked back to check on Ninnis and were shocked to see no trace of him.

Ninnis had plunged on into the abyss along with the bulk of their equipment and rations.

Mawson and Mertz now faced getting back to base, 850 kilometres away. They had enough food for 10 or 11 days. Two weeks after they left the crevasse, both men were suffering from violent diarrhoea, scaling skin and sores, and infected fingers and toes. Mertz fell into a coma and died. Mawson was scarcely better off. In his journal Mawson recorded: *The sight of my feet gave me quite a shock, for the thickened skin of the soles had separated in each case as a complete layer, and abundant fluid had escaped into the socks. The new skin underneath was very abraded and raw.*

A week later, crossing a glacier, Mawson himself plunged through the ice and into an abyss. His sledge, however, jammed at the lip. Mawson, attached to it by a rope, found himself dangling, alive, but with the sledge slowly slipping towards the edge.

Mawson strained to reach a knot in the rope. And then another. Painfully, he hauled himself close to the surface. He was home free! And then part of the lip gave way and he plunged down once more.

He hung there in despair, but Mawson was not a man to give up. *'It was the occasion for a supreme attempt. New power seemed to come as I addressed myself to one last tremendous effort. The struggle occupied some time, but by a miracle I rose slowly to the surface.'* He rested, and decided, he tells us in the journal, *'to plug on'.*

On 29 January 1913 Mawson was down to his last kilogram of food and at least a week away from base. In an incredible stroke of fortune, he spotted black bunting (a collection of cloth ribbons) on a snow mound, and beneath it was a bag of food left by a search party from Commonwealth Bay. With the food was a note telling Mawson that 30 kilometres away he would find more food in *'Aladdin's Cave'* and that the expedition ship, the *Aurora*, would wait for him until the last moment.

On his hands and knees, pulling his sledge, Mawson made it to the cave three days later. He had hardly thrown himself into the warmth of its shelter when a hurricane hit and raged for a week while Mawson gathered his strength. A week later, Mawson reached Commonwealth Bay. The *Aurora* had just left for Australia before winter set in, but five of his fellow explorers had volunteered to stay on to wait for the return of Mawson and his party.

Ten months later Mawson sailed back to Australia where he was knighted and showered with honours. But the fascination with Antarctica, had ebbed now that the nation was on the brink of war.

Douglas Mawson's epic of courage and endurance coincided with the advent of the First World War and passed without the acclaim it deserved. Most Australians today only have a vague notion of Mawson's extraordinary achievements in two fields: science and exploration. Despite Mawson's great contribution to Australia, this hero's story has remained relatively unsung.

• JAMES MONTAGU SMITH •

After committing sundry rows and breaches of the peace, such as blowing up the seat of the privy [toilet] and bringing rum in to school in coconuts…I got expelled and sent to my Guardian, Mr Hay.

That was how James Montagu Smith began his memoirs of life in Australia in the 1850s. Mostly an account of his teenage years, it's a story that few teenagers today could imagine.

Twice imprisoned and almost lost at sea, James was frequently in scrapes because he would not back away when he felt he was in the right. James, nonetheless, was a young adventurer whose decency, strong social conscience and fierce love for his adopted country stamped him as a model of the Australian who was to emerge in coming generations. His enthralling memoirs remained known only to his descendants until 1996, when they were chanced upon and later published under the title *Send the Boy to Sea: The Memoirs of a Sailor on the Goldfields* (The Five Mile Press).

Before he was 21, James had made three voyages halfway round the world. On his first, on board *The Lancastrian*, bound for Melbourne, the 14-year-old quickly found himself in trouble and was punished by being tied to the ship's sails high above the deck. On another voyage, James was handcuffed to the mast in freezing weather and then locked up in the Black Box: '*…like a coffin standing on its end – one can neither sit or lie, nor indeed stand comfortably.*'

In Hobart Town a callous magistrate ordered James to be put on the '*treadmill*', where '*a great many men were walking up a large wheel, apparently very uselessly, for they never got any higher. We were told to get up. It was very difficult at first, for we were frequently missing the steps and hurting our shins.'*

Released and at sea again, James sailed from the convict colony at Norfolk Island – *'a perfect little paradise inhabited by demons'* – on a ship with 300 convicts below deck. The convicts broke out and were in hiding ready to overpower the ship's officers and marines when a cabin boy spotted one of them. The boy kept quiet until he could alert the captain, and the savage melee ended with the marines firing blanks into the convicts' midst.

Returned to Hobart Town, James escaped his ship but was caught and returned and put in solitary confinement: *'the punishment most dreaded…a stone cell, perfectly dark, very very very very cold – only one blanket allowed at night…and…half a pound of bread per day… No man could endure it for any length of time.'*

The year 1853 found James digging for gold and joining other miners in their fight against the hated gold-mining licence. *'It is paid willingly by none except the very timid… The troopers are mounted and well armed with carbine, sword and pistols which they are allowed to use when called on.'* And he went on, prophetically: *'These diabolic proceedings… will some time or other cause them to repent it.'* James left the goldfields just nine days before the slaughter at Eureka Stockade in December of 1854.

James felt suffocated by the class system or his native England, with its stuffiness and hypocrisy. He hated the way young English middle-class women were kept powerless – used as objects for profitable marriage matches, knowing little and doing less. And he sympathised with and admired the Aborigines. *'They…prefer God's canopy to Man's, and for this they are called barbarians; and for this they are despised. Pshaw!'* he wrote in disgust.

A fervent believer in mateship and a fair go, and passionate about his adopted country, James was the sort of man – brave, adventurous and proud – who would land at Gallipoli half a century on. A forgotten hero.

• MATTHEW FLINDERS •

For more than six years, and at the height of his fame, Matthew Flinders was held prisoner on an island, and all because he refused an invitation to dinner. The intriguing question of history is – what might Flinders have done had he not been so foolish?

Flinders' writing tells us much about the man. He was ambitious to an extraordinary degree. Flinders wanted to be famous – very famous. *'I have too much ambition to rest in the unnoticed middle-order of mankind,'* he wrote to Sir Joseph Banks. *'...I cannot rival the immortalised name of Cook, yet if persevering industry joined to what ability I may possess, can accomplish it, then I will secure the second place.'*

Flinders was born in 1774, and when he was 14 he enlisted in the navy. Six years later, his ship, the *Bellerophon*, was in the thick of it at the Battle of Brest. The *Bellerophon* took a fearful battering from the French. Its commander had a leg blown away, and all around him Flinders saw his shipmates torn to tatters. He noted all he saw, and his 40-page account is considered to be the best individual record of the battle.

The year after the momentous Battle of Brest, Flinders, now Master's Mate, joined the *Reliance* on the journey to New South Wales with the new governor, Hunter. On the voyage, Flinders won the approval of Hunter and the friendship of the ship's surgeon, 25-year-old George Bass. The two shared a passion for geographic discovery. Together, and sometimes individually, they explored and charted much of the coast south of Sydney in Bass's small boat, the *Tom Thumb*. In 1798 they set out to prove their theory that Van Diemen's Land (renamed Tasmania in 1855) was an island. They believed that ships would cut a week or more from the passage from England by passing between it and the mainland of Australia (as Flinders later named the continent). The pair circumnavigated the island and Governor Hunter named the strait, at Flinders' recommendation, after Bass. Then Flinders and Bass parted.

Flinders, now a lieutenant, made further exploratory voyages along the east coast of Australia, where his journals and meticulous navigation charts stamped him as a man with a brilliant future. By the time he returned to England (and soon after married his childhood sweetheart, Ann Chapell), Flinders was 26.

In 1801 Flinders, already acknowledged as one of the finest marine navigators, was poised for the immortality he craved. He was given the *Investigator* and ordered to explore the coast between Van Diemen's Land and Western Australia. Flinders sailed on around Australia, but the *Investigator*'s timbers were rotten. He was returning to England to get a better vessel when the ship struck a reef off the Queensland coast and sank. With a skeleton crew, Flinders took a cutter and found his way back to Sydney to arrange the rescue of those left behind.

From Sydney, Flinders set out on his fateful voyage. Sailing in a schooner that began leaking badly, he stopped at the French island of Mauritius. There he learned that, once again, England and France were at war, and the French governor suspected he might be a spy. The governor questioned the Englishman at length but then, satisfied, invited Flinders to join him at dinner. Flinders, in a moment of arrogant stupidity, stood on his dignity and declined. The governor immediately placed him under arrest.

Six and a half years later Flinders was released and sailed for England. He was broken in health and died, aged 40, the day after his monumental work *A Voyage to Terra Australis* was published.

• GEORGE BASS •

Like his friend Matthew Flinders, George Bass seemed on the verge of great things when fate took a hand and he disappeared into the mists of history. Just what happened to Bass will never be known. Most likely his ship was lost at sea. But there is every chance that he was killed by pirates. George Bass, 32, had been warned to look out for Spanish pirates when he left Sydney in 1803 bound for Chile. Those warnings would not have deterred Bass. He was, said a friend, *'fond of enterprise and despising danger in every shape'.*

The voyage around Tasmania he made in 1798 with Flinders is Bass's most momentous achievement, but perhaps his greatest triumph was in the way he lived his life. George Bass was an adventurer of the highest order. He was 18 when he joined the navy as a surgeon's mate in 1789 and spent the next five years in postings on several ships until he found himself on the *Reliance* sailing for New South Wales. On board, too, was Matthew Flinders. Like Bass, Flinders was a voracious reader and a romantic, yearning for adventure and exploration.

Seven weeks after arriving in Sydney on the *Reliance*, Bass and Flinders set out in a small rowing boat with a mast attached and charted the surrounding area. Botany Bay, Port Jackson and Broken Bay had already been charted, but the coast between Jervis Bay, to the south of Sydney, and Port Stephens, to the north, was little known. In the tiny boat *Tom Thumb*, with Bass's boy-servant William Martin, Bass and Flinders undertook a remarkable and often dangerous feat of coastal navigation.

In 1798, in the sloop *Norfolk*, the pair sailed around Van Diemen's

Land, proving that there was a strait between it and the mainland. The voyage had a number of important results. It showed that ships need not sail round the south of Van Diemen's Land on the voyages from England to Sydney. Also, Bass established through his field studies that the island was ideal for colonisation. Importantly, Bass took copious notes of the flora and fauna – he was particularly fascinated by wombats, one of which he caught and tried to tame – and he tried to communicate with the Aboriginal inhabitants.

Flinders gives this account of a meeting with an Aborigine:

He was of middle age, unarmed except with a whaddie or wooden scimitar, and came to us seemingly with careless confidence. We made much of him, and gave him some biscuit; and he in return presented us with a piece of gristly fat, probably of a whale. This I tasted but watching an opportunity to spit it out when he should not be looking, I perceived him doing precisely the same thing with our biscuit, whose taste was probably no more agreeable to him than his whale was to me.

From a young age Bass had been fascinated by the South Pacific, and when he was given 12 months' leave by the navy, sailed trading ships between the islands. He fell in love, married and was with his wife for only 10 weeks when, deeply in debt, he set sail to find a market in Chile for goods he could not sell in Sydney. Bass was never seen again. All that can be said with certainty is that whatever happened to him, George Bass would have gone down fighting.

• ADAM GILCHRIST •

Sixteen-year-old Adam Gilchrist, destined to be the most terrifying batsman international cricket has known, used to weep from loneliness. The gangling boy with the flyaway ears had left school in Australia and gone to seek his cricketing fortune in England. In the loft bedroom of his hosts' home, he missed his family in Deniliquin, New South Wales. Across the other side of the world his close-knit family missed him too.

Adam's dad Stan was a schoolteacher and a cricket coach. All the Gilchrist kids – three boys and Jacki, the eldest – followed Dad on to the field when it came time to play on Saturday arvo. It was Stan who taught them that if you were going to hit the ball, hit it hard.

Adam did that. The first man to hit 100 sixes in Test cricket, the second-fastest scorer of a Test cricket century, 'Gilly' consistently smacked a cricket ball harder than anyone. When he retired, in January 2008, he was universally hailed as the greatest wicketkeeper–batsman the game has known. Many, like the former England keeper Alec Stewart, called him the *'the greatest all-rounder the game has ever seen'*. His colleagues, past and present Australian Test cricketers, voted him the best batsman in one-day internationals. Richie Benaud, the game's venerable and venerated commentator, said he had never seen a man hit a ball with such timing. Steve Waugh said he was *'the complete package. A once in a generation genius.'*

High praise. But more than that, Adam Gilchrist changed the way Test cricket had been played for more than 130 years. Before Gilchrist exploded on to the international stage in 1999, wicketkeepers were almost always stumpy men who came in to bat for an entertaining half an hour or so, during which they would swish hit and/or miss and walk off with their reputation and their batting average of around 26 safely secure.

Gilchrist swished, but he seldom missed. And when he walked off, usually caught trying to hit another six, it was with his average of around 52 safely intact. In the time he was at the crease the game, so often, was turned on its head. Australia might be struggling with five wickets lost for a total of 150 or so and facing certain defeat, just as we were in Gilchrist's second Test, in Hobart, in 1999. Australia was five for 226, chasing 369 to beat Pakistan when Gilchrist and Justin Langer combined for a 238-run partnership. Gilchrist hit 149 not out from 163 balls.

From then on, Gilchrist did it again and again: saved Australia from looming disaster and turned the game into a crushing victory. A grateful captain, Ricky Ponting, said, *'Gilchrist revolutionised the way wicketkeepers play.'*

'He is a different type of opponent,' said India's Test captain Anil Kumble. *'A very nice man, humble, straightforward and down to earth. He came across as someone who cared and he made the extra effort to show it.'*

Gilchrist showed he cared when he wore a set of pink gloves at the MCG to support breast-cancer research, and as vice-captain of Australia he chose to miss the start of the 2007 World Cup so that he could be at the birth of his third child, Archie. Australia might have been in trouble if Archie had taken his time arriving. But all went well and Gilchrist arrived in time to see the team through to the finals, where he hammered 149 from 104 deliveries as Australia beat Sri Lanka in Barbados. (He had done much the same in the 1999 World Cup final, where his assault on Pakistan's tearaway fast bowler Shoaib Akhtar set up Australia's victory.)

There has never been one like him, and there may never be again. *'As a cricketer he was a great man, and, as men go, he was a great cricketer,'* said the Australian's Peter Lalor. *'Gilchrist seemed to be the last great folk hero.'*

• EDWIN FLACK •

TED'S EXCELLENT ADVENTURE

Edwin Flack is – just – remembered as our first Olympic gold medallist, the winner of two gold medals at the first modern Olympic Games in Athens in 1896. Accounts of his wins emphasise the haphazard nature of his entry – he just turned up on a whim – and the distinctly amateur flavour of the Games; but in truth the Games were fiercely contended before huge crowds.

For instance, When Spiridon Louis, an Athens post office messenger, tottered to the line to win the marathon, 70,000 spectators went wild. Greek royalty ran to greet him, women flung jewels at his feet, a man offered Spiridon his daughter's hand in marriage and a million drachmas to go with her. Edwin – Teddy as he was known – was in that race and had led towards the finish before exhaustion overtook him.

Small wonder Teddy Flack had been busy since the Games' opening day.

A Melbourne accountant based in London where he was a member of three running clubs, Teddy went to Athens intrigued by the concept of the Games instigator, Baron de Coubertin, and the prospect of having a go. He packed his running shoes, shorts and vest just in case and set sail. Six days later he was in the Olympic city and five days later he was putting on his shoes, shorts and vest and running, on the opening day, in a heat of the 800 metres.

Teddy won easily. The next day Teddy decided to have a go at the 1500. He won that easily in a time of four minutes, 32.2 seconds, the first of dozens of gold medals – actually, the first-place medals were silver then – Australia would win over the next century.

The next day he played tennis and finished third in the doubles. He was bundled out in the first round of the singles – probably just as well, because after lunch he had to compete in the final of the 800. He won that, in a time of two minutes, 11.9 seconds.

What to do now? Teddy immediately hopped into a carriage and started off for Marathon, four hours away. The next day he was off and running well but three-quarters of the way through the race, and leading, he got the wobbles. He'd never run longer than 15 kilometres and the 42.195-kilometre race was just too far for a man who'd won the 800-metre and 1500-metre races on the days before. And played a bit of tennis in between.

Still, Teddy Flack will always be the only man ever to win Olympic medals for track and field and tennis, and to have competed in four events over three days.

• WALLY LEWIS •

> THE KING

Cometh the hour, cometh the man. It's an age-old saying and it sounds impressive, but what, actually, does it mean?

Well, take the case of Wally Lewis. Wally Lewis was a supremely gifted member of the Australian Schoolboys Rugby Union side that toured Europe, Britain and Japan in 1977–78, sweeping all before it. In the same side were the Ella brothers and other soon-to-be-notable union players. But injury and the selectors' preference for the brilliant Mark Ella meant the young Queenslander missed many games and he decided to switch codes.

In April 1978 Wally Lewis went over to rugby league. Almost immediately he made his mark, earning the Brisbane Colt of the Year award and maturing just in time to take part in the league's new State of Origin series.

State of Origin football, where players are selected to play for the state in which they made their senior football debut, was not a new concept. The Australian Football League had staged State of Origin game before crowds of up to 90,000. The AFL fans loved State of Origin but the coaches and the players disliked it: it got in the way of the premiership competition and the advent of the national competition saw its end.

Rugby league, however, after initial scepticism and resistance from New South Wales, decided to give State of Origin football a trial. In 1980, in the first, historic, Origin game, Wally Lewis made an unremarkable debut. The following year, however, Lewis, now captain of the Maroons, sensationally turned the game around, taking his team from 15-0 down to a 22-15 win. Queenslanders went bananas. For years they had watched their best players, most of them stars of the competition in Sydney, turn out for New South Wales. Each year it was a ritual, humiliating, thumping of the Queensland players who had not gone south.

But now the boot was on the other foot. And the boot belonged to the man they came to call *'the King',* Wally Lewis. Queensland's 1981 miracle comeback was the beginning of 10 phenomenal years when Wally Lewis won eight man of the match awards in Origin games. Along the way he changed the way rugby league was played and took it from its parochial past, a game enjoyed in only two states, to the national sports calendar. Today, around the nation, State of Origin is compulsory viewing for millions of football fans of all codes.

• CASEY STONER •

He looks like the kid who gets pushed around in the schoolyard. He's slightly built and has a slightly goofy grin. But beneath that mild-mannered exterior is a millionaire man of steel: an incredibly courageous sportsman who is the best in his business – and his business is the dangerous but thrilling world of MotoGP.

In 2007, babyfaced Casey Stoner won the world championship. It was something he had been headed for since his first race on a motorbike at the age of four at his Kurri Kurri, New South Wales home. He won his first race in the under-nines category at the Hatcher's dirt racing track on the Gold Coast and, two years later, he had won his first Australian title. For the next eight years, travelling with his father, mother and sister, Casey competed in motorbike races around Australia, winning 41 Australian dirt and long track titles and over 70 state titles.

By 14 he was riding overseas and working his way to the top. It was tough going for the teenager and his family, who had to scrape to keep Casey competing. And there was the matter of his riding style. Casey was fast, but he had a habit of coming off his bikes. That was all right with Casey. You can't teach a slow rider to go fast, but you can teach a fast reader how to avoid coming off.

In his first year, after just one race in England, he won immediate sponsorship and went on to take out the English 125cc Aprilia Championship in 2000. In that year the Grand Prix legend Alberto Puig saw him ride in Spain and invited him to race for the Telefonica Movistar Team in the 125cc Spanish Championships the next year. It was the start of a steady climb up the classes.

In 2005 Casey finished second in the 250cc class and in 2007 Casey, now with Italy's revered Ducati, was riding in the tracks of Australian legends Wayne Gardner and Mick Doohan, competing in the fastest and most prestigious of all the classes, the MotoGP.

It had taken him just six years to get to the top – and just one season to finish as world champion. On 23 September 2007, at the Japanese Grand Prix, 21-year-old Casey Stoner became the first rider in over 30 years to win the MotoGP title on a European-made bike and the second-youngest World Champion in the MotoGP category.

• RICKY PONTING •

> MEETING TRIUMPH AND DISASTER <

Ricky Ponting was a teenager when Australia's wicketkeeper Rod Marsh encountered him. Marsh was astounded. Ponting, he said, was the finest batsman of his age. And the talk began that one day the baby-faced lad from Launceston would captain Australia.

Ponting lived for cricket. He relished fast bowling and played it with elegant pulls, hooks and square cuts. In the field he was dazzling: catching in close or throwing down stumps, Ponting could do it all – even bowl a respectable medium pace when called upon. He had the skills to play for Australia. But did he have the temperament to follow in the steps of Steve Waugh, Ian Chappell, Richie Benaud, Don Bradman and on down the line to 1877 and the first of Australia's Test captains, Dave Gregory?

The answer to that question took some time to come. Ponting was just 20 when he made his Test debut in 1995. Very few Australians have made it to the top at that age – Bradman himself had to wait until he was 21 before donning the Baggy Green cap. Unlike Bradman, whose first game for Australia was undistinguished, Ponting made an immediate impact, unluckily given out when on 96.

But also unlike Bradman, Ricky Ponting had problems with discipline and form. Off the field the brilliant young batsman was sometimes far from impressive. There was an incident in a bar that left him with a black eye, and Ponting admitted he had an alcohol problem. He was dropped from the Test side after 22 games and an average of just 36.63.

That might have been the end of it. He would not have been

the first prodigy to fail. Ian Craig, another brilliant young batsman, had made history when he was given his Test cap at 17 and went on to captain Australia before the burden of being hailed as the next Bradman coupled with ill health caused his career to self-destruct almost overnight.

Ponting, however, met the challenges. He matured, and he stayed out of trouble. In 2002 he was given the captaincy of Australia's One Day International team, married his long-time girlfriend, Rianna, and led Australia to the 2003 World Cup crown, making a blazing 140 in the final. Ponting was on top of the world.

In 2004, when Steve Waugh retired, Ponting was the unanimous choice for captain of the Test team. Almost at once came disaster. Australia lost the 2005 Ashes, a catastrophe that had the nation reeling. And Ponting, many said, was to blame. Despite his valiant batting the skipper was criticised for sending England in to bat in the Second Test, a Test Australia lost, along with the series, 2–1.

The next year England toured Australia and the matches were expected to be as keenly fought as the 2005 Ashes series. Brilliantly led by Ponting, Man of the Series, Australia reclaimed the Ashes 5–0.

Ricky Ponting's batting record is surpassed only by Bradman and Tendulkar. As a captain he shares with Steve Waugh the distinction of having led his side to 16 consecutive victories. But his greatest triumph may be in the way he has overcome the disciplinary and personal problems that threatened his career.

Ricky Ponting's success, on field and off, is a resounding echo of Rudyard Kipling's famous lines:

If you can meet with Triumph and Disaster and treat those two impostors just the same…you'll be a man my son.

• ROD LAVER •

Back in the 1920s the Chicago chewing-gum moneybags William Wrigley Junior thought it would be a good idea to name the Chicago Cubs' stadium Wrigley Fields. Since he also owned the club, the Cubs couldn't have agreed more, and Wrigley Fields it remains to this day.

Wrigley was the first to have naming rights to a stadium.

Today it's commonplace. Around the world cities and clubs have sold the naming rights to stadiums. It's a commercial decision. Sport must have sponsors and sponsors must have naming rights. (Mind you, you can go too far with this. The famous old English club Ipswich Town ran a competition with the winner having a stand named after him or her. The club's North Stand was renamed the Sandra Cunningham Stand.)

But major sports stadiums named after sports stars are surprisingly rare. Detroit has Joe Louis Arena, known as The Joe, and named after the great heavyweight boxer. In Austria there's Arnold Schwarzenegger Stadium, whether because he was once a body builder – if that is a sport – or because he was a movie star turned politician is not known. But the fact remains, stadiums named after stars are few: you have to be someone to have a stadium named after you. Rod Laver is someone.

The Rod Laver Arena in Melbourne Park, home of the Australian Open tennis tournament, is a state-of-the-art 15,000-seat arena with a retractable roof. Each year the world's best players compete there for the title of Open champion. And each year the greats talk of their favourite players. Rod Laver's name comes up more than anyone's.

The third son of a central Queensland farmer, Rod Laver grew up with two older brothers, much older, much bigger and much stronger than the redheaded tyke who tried to take them on at tennis. They were better at tennis, too; among the best players in the state. So Rod learned to survive, first by keeping the ball in play – *'You try not to make errors. Losers make the errors'* – and then, slowly, as he grew older, by guile and skill. Finally, the strength came.

Laver was nicknamed 'Rocket' by Harry Hopman, his coach. Hopman was being ironic. A notoriously hard task-master, he thought young Rod was a little lazy. But Laver could equally have been nicknamed Popeye. Though he is relatively short, at 172 centimetres, his left forearm, developed from hitting thousands of tennis balls, is the size of a heavyweight boxer's. Combined with his compact build, his agility and speed around the court, it gave Laver an edge that won him four Wimbledon, three Australian, two US and two French Open titles. He twice won the Grand Slam (the four major tennis titles), the only player to do this.

Laver might have won the Grand Slam a third or even fourth time. For five years, he was out of the circuit while competing on the professional tour. He had been by far the best amateur in the world, but the professionals, he found, were a class above. Still, by the end of his first year he was holding his own, and from 1964 through to 1967 he won the World Professional Indoor Tournament. In 1968, when the amateur and professional worlds got together, he won Wimbledon once again.

He was the undisputed champ. And he remains the man most admired for his demeanour – quiet, modest and courteous – on and off court. A true sportsman.

And that's another reason to name a stadium after him.

• PETER THOMSON •

> THE GREATEST

On and off, Peter Thomson has been writing about and commentating on golf for almost half a century. In that time he has hailed a number of emerging Australian golfers – Greg Norman, Robert Allenby and Adam Scott in particular – and accurately predicated their future success. But in 2008 he made a rare error of judgement. Thomson nominated Karrie Webb, the former women's world number-one golfer, as the finest Australia has produced.

The finest Australian golfer, and one of the world's all-time greatest, is Peter Thomson. Thomson won the British Open five times, and was three times runner-up. Greg Norman won the Open twice. They were both champions, but what was the difference between the two? *'The super player has one vital quality,'* Thomson once said. *'Calmness.'*

Calmness is what's needed on the last day and the back nine of a major championship. Greg Norman was rarely calm on the inward nine of an Open. You could see the wheels fall off. Thomson, on the other hand, was icy cool. His starts to tournaments were often nothing startling, but his finishes were lethal. In the 1950s, in Britain, they terrified his opponents. There seemed no way that he wasn't going to win, or at least finish ahead of them.

Consider his Open record from 1951. Including his five wins and three seconds, he finished out of the top 10 just three times over 20 years.

It was said by some – Americans in the main – that Thomson owed his spectacular success in Europe to the lack of opposition from the top US players. He disproved that at Royal Birkdale in 1965 when, in swirling winds, he beat the defending champion from the US, Tony Lema, and a field that included the world's top three players, Jack Nicklaus, Arnold Palmer and Lema.

Thomson disliked playing the American tour, but finished tied fourth in the US Open and fifth in the Masters, events that he contested only a handful of times. In 1956, playing in just eight events, he finished in the top 10 on the US money list.

Three decades later, in 1985, Thomson returned to the US to compete on the Seniors PGA Tour. He won nine tournaments and finished top of the money list. His last tournament victory came at the 1988 British PGA Seniors Championship, when he was inducted into golf's Hall of Fame.

Australia's best golfer? The record speaks for itself.

• KEVIN SHEEDY •

> THE SOFT CENTRE OF A HARD NUT <

He was a hard-nut footballer – when you collided with Richmond's Kevin Sheedy you felt as if he'd brought his plumbing tool bag with him. In the 1970s, when their team barnstormed to premierships, Tiger fans bellowed: *'Eat 'em alive!'* And Kevin Sheedy, it seemed, did his best to do so. He was never better than on a *'big game'*, when his take-no-prisoners attitude had opposition players looking nervously over their shoulders.

Other fans hated Sheedy. The day he retired was a day of great rejoicing. He might have gone on with his plumbing job and slipped into obscurity but in 1981, Essendon, one of the AFL's powerhouse teams, asked him to coach. They wanted a man who could give the team the bite that wins premierships. It was the beginning of a 27-year partnership with the club that saw it win four flags in 19 finals campaigns and the respect – even, astonishingly, affection – of football fans from all clubs.

In his last home game 88,468 farewelled *'Sheeds'* and veteran star player James Hird with a standing ovation. They applauded Sheedy, not for his success with Essendon, but for his greater contribution to football and to Australia. Sheedy's ideas are innovative and, sometimes, it seems, a little wacky. But he shaped modern AFL football more than any other. And more than any other, he brought indigenous footballers into the game. He believes that football's Aboriginal stars bring hope and inspiration to young Aborigines.

For most of its 150 years Australian football at the highest level was played almost exclusively by whites. But in the last quarter of a century hundreds of indigenous footballers have made the trip to the big cities to play in the big league. In 2008 there were 72 listed with the 17 clubs – eight of them with Essendon, which, under Sheedy, has led the way. Today 10 per cent of the total number of listed footballers are indigenous – and within the next decade that number is likely to double.

That is Sheeds' lasting legacy.

• GREG NORMAN •

For 12 years, regular as clockwork – alarm clocks were set for around 5.30 or six in the morning – the television set was turned on early in millions of homes around Australia. And millions of men, women and children ate their breakfast, skipped the newspaper and missed their trains as they watched Greg Norman lose another Major.

Golf has four annual 'Majors' championships: the US Open, the US PGA, the Augusta Masters and the British Open. Each year for more than a decade, and at almost every Major, you could count on Greg Norman being in contention to win. That's a total of 48 Majors. He finished in the top 10 on no fewer than 29 occasions. But he won only two.

Greg Norman might have won – with a bit of luck, more nerve and less adrenalin – as many as eight Majors. But though he was – for a decade, before Tiger Woods came on the scene – the world's top golfer, winner of more than 70 tournaments worldwide, he just couldn't win the big ones. Too often, we finally had to admit, he *'choked'*.

In 1986, he led all four Majors – the Grand Slam – after the third round of four rounds but won only the British Open. (Cruel commentators call this the Norman Slam: leading after the third round on Saturday but losing in the final round on Sunday.) And he is one of only two players to have competed in and lost play-offs in all four of the Majors.

But the most embarrassing Norman meltdown of all, the greatest calamity in golf history, was his loss to arch rival Nick Faldo at the 1996 Masters. Norman's opening three rounds at Augusta that year gave him a seemingly choke-proof lead of six shots. No one with such a lead had ever lost before. Norman did it. And what's more, he managed to lose by the amazing margin of five shots – an 11-shot turnaround over 18 holes.

So why is Greg Norman in this book? Because though he lost, he never lost it: he never threw tantrums, sulked or whinged. He kept his dignity no matter what. After the greatest meltdown golf has known he could smile ruefully as he told reporters, *'I'd love to be up there putting that [winner's] green jacket on, but it's not the end of the world. I'm disappointed, I'm sad about it because I know I let it slip away, it's not the end of my life.'*

Norman's acceptance sparked a flood of thousands of letters from well wishers, something he claimed was a transforming experience. Good looking, charismatic, and with the ability to hit the ball far beyond most others, Norman himself transformed golf. He made it much more popular, particularly in Australia where he inspired a generation of young golfers, half a dozen of them now ranked in the world top 50, and in the years of his dominance golf-club membership in Australia rose almost 40 per cent.

Norman has been a wonderful ambassador for Australia. Former US president George Bush, father of George W, said it for many around the world: *'Greg Norman is a true legend to the game of golf. I am proud to consider him a friend. He has shown all golf fans an awful lot of class, both in victory and defeat. They broke the mould when they made this golf legend.'*

• DON BRADMAN •

The story goes that Sir Donald Bradman, who had retired 40 years before with a Test batting average of 99.94, was asked how he thought he would fare against the bowlers of the late 1980s. What might his average be?

Bradman thought about it. *'Well it's very hard to say, but probably it'd be about the 75-run mark... Mind you, I'm over 80 years old now.'*

Does any batsman past or present approach Bradman? In 1996, watching the World Cup on television, Bradman called for his wife Jessie to come and see the young Indian batting genius Sachin Tendulkar, saying: *'I never saw myself play, but I feel like this young man is playing the way I used to play.'*

Bradman himself told the story of how he had called for his wife to see Tendulkar, saying, *'Who does he remind you of?'* But, says Colin McDonald, an opener for Australia who played in the twilight of Bradman's career, this just isn't so.

'Bradman was wrong,' McDonald told the Age. *'Tendulkar is a textbook batsman, the sort coaches salivate about. But Bradman didn't bat anything like him. Most balls to Bradman were bad balls – to him, not to others. He played strokes no one else would think of playing. The good ball to Bradman was despatched. Only the very good ball forced him to defend.'*

Bill O'Reilly, the man Bradman rated as the best bowler he'd faced, had his differences with the *'Little Master'* on a personal level. But this is how he rated Bradman: *'There's never been and never will be, in my estimation, a batsman so good as that fellow. Bradman was a bloke whose ability with the bat was inconceivable...a modern miracle.'*

Bradman was never coached; he was never so much as told how to hold a bat. *'I was my own teacher, and the first bat I ever used was the limb of a gum tree. No boy lived near enough to my home to join me in a game, and often as not I was left to play alone.'* His next 'bat' was a cricket stump, and in the backyard of his Bowral, New South Wales, home, he'd use it to a hit a golf ball against a corrugated-iron water tank. Hour after hour he'd practice, refining his hand–eye co-ordination against balls that came back to him fast and hard and from all angles.

In 1921, aged 13, he was playing for Bowral, wielding a real cricket bat and using it like a real batsman. Coming in at eighth wicket down, he made 37 not out and Bowral won the game. Nine years later, at Leeds and coming in at number three for Australia, he made 300 not out in one day. Australia won that match, too. For the next 30 years few teams with Bradman in the line-up didn't win.

Bradman came at just the right moment in our history. When he made his astounding triple century at Leeds against England, the Depression that gripped Australia and the terrible legacy of the Great War that cost 60,000 Australian lives were forgotten.

In his final test match, in 1948, Bradman needed to make just four runs for the dream average of 100. He was bowled, second ball, for a duck. Ironically, that failure only added to the legend. No man or woman has ever been so dominant in a major international sport and it's said that, still, at any time of the day or night someone, somewhere, is talking about Don Bradman.

• BARRY HUMPHRIES •

THE INIMITABLE

Barry Humphries was born to be bad. The first son of a well-off Melbourne family, he was spoiled – rotten – all throughout his young life. When he left school he found himself at a loss to know what to do and for a time he was employed at a recording company with the sole task of smashing outdated vinyl records with a hammer.

Since then, of course, he has smashed records all over the world. His shows are sellouts from London to New York and scores of cities in between. He is the most successful solo stage performer in the world. (Hey, do you think Madonna will still be performing in her 70s?)

Humphries' characters – the appalling Dame Edna Everage, the revolting Dr Sir Leslie Colin Patterson (Les Patterson) and the sweet old soul Sandy Stone – are masterpieces of comedy. But even if he'd remained with the record company, still smashing vinyl at the age of 70-something, Barry Humphries would be a peerless comedian, and his comedy is based on being bad.

He can't help himself. Long before he went on the stage Barry was performing, often for his own amusement. As a schoolboy at Melbourne Grammar he'd go into a shop and buy a cake of soap. When the shopkeeper gave it to him Barry would pay for it, then hand it back and say, *'Oh no thanks. I don't want the soap. I just wanted to buy it.'* Then he'd make his exit, leaving the shopkeeper with a story that would be retold for years.

At university he had plenty of accomplices to help his practical-joke routines. His classic was The Travelling Breakfast. Barry would arrange for a string of accomplices to be stationed at stops along a suburban train route, each waiting at the end of the platform. Barry would board the last carriage of the train half a dozen stops from the city.

At the first stop he would be met by an accomplice with the newspapers, a napkin and cutlery. Barry would accept them without comment and the train would start off again. At the next stop there was a glass of orange juice and a small serve of grapefruit. At the next, cereal. Then eggs and bacon. Finally, coffee. And as the train pulled in to the city, someone to take his breakfast away.

That never failed to have the passengers speechless.

When he was able to afford to fly he liked to board with a can of mixed carrots and peas, or – even better – coleslaw. Once in the air Barry would surreptitiously open the can and empty it into the brown paper sick bag in the seat pocket. Then he'd begin to make small, but disturbing, barfing noises. When he had the full attention of passengers around him he'd bury his head in the bag. Then he'd straighten up, take from his pocket a spoon and – well, you can guess the rest.

For a long time critics of Humphries said his characters belittled Australia. They don't of course. People laugh at Edna and Les because they recognise one of their own. Humour is universal, and few artists are as funny as Barry Humphries.

• PERCY GRAINGER •

Australia's most eminent composer, and one of our greatest pianists, Percy Grainger was also an outstanding eccentric. Everything about Percy Grainger was eccentric. If it wasn't, he made sure it was! He was diminutive, only 160 centimetres tall, but he brushed his wild red hair so high that it added an extra 20 centimetres or so. He designed his own clothes – clothes that would be considered now as ultracontemporary and chic: puff-sleeved jackets with multicoloured panels, white linen trousers – or, often, shorts – and tan military boots of the Doc Martens variety.

Some of Percy's clothes are on display in the Percy Grainger Museum at Melbourne University. There are, too, his mother's clothes, locks of his hair, and thousands of letters, books, tapes, recordings and sheet music. There are pianos, an early Edison phonograph and his unique free-form music machines – devices made from *'found objects'* like brown paper rolls, valves and pulleys.

Percy Grainger was born in Melbourne in 1882. His parents separated in 1890 and his mother raised him with almost obsessive devotion. He was a child prodigy, giving concerts from an early age, the proceeds of which helped support them, his estranged father and others. For most of his life, the need to support up to nine people kept Percy on the concert-hall circuit when he should have been free to compose.

Percy liked innovation in music: *'Audiences only like music they know. How can they get a thrill out of it when they know what's coming up all the time?'* And he pronounced American jazz-band leader Duke Ellington one of the three greatest composers who ever lived. (The other two were Bach and Delius.)

Percy Grainger loved the sensation he caused when he appeared on the concert platform. He was a star, and he behaved like one. He often appeared at concerts with only seconds to spare, having hiked many kilometres to the concert hall with a rucksack on his back. He didn't care for the starched shirts and tails of the concert pianist. He never ironed his shirts and washed all his clothes in the hotel bedroom basin, explaining: *It's quicker that way. Don't even have to iron the shirts – they don't show from the stage, you know.*

In Australia, Percy's fame was far less than it was in America, where he lived from 1914 and where he was held in the highest esteem. He became an American citizen, reluctantly, *I am bitterly ashamed of having to change my nationality,'* he once stated. Above all, he wanted to be acknowledged as an Australian composer. One of his Australian-inspired compositions, The Warriors, an Aboriginal ballet, was written for three grand pianos and a full symphony orchestra. It was performed in Chicago with no fewer than 19 pianos.

Percy Grainger was a close friend of two great composers, Delius and Grieg. Greig, the great Norwegian composer, said of Percy Grainger:

As a piano player which of the very greatest I should liken him to. But all comparison is futile when greatness is the question... If I had his technique my conception of the nature of piano playing would have been exactly the same. Like a God he is lifted above all suffering, all struggle. But one feels they have been there, but are overcome. It is a man, a great and distinguished man who plays. May life go well for him.

In 1928 Grainger and Ella Strom married in front of 30,000 people at the Hollywood Bowl. Percy died in 1961 at his New York home, but his heart was always in Australia.

• LACHLAN MACQUARIE •

> TURNING THE COLONY INTO AUSTRALIA <

Governor Lachlan Macquarie devoted his time in New South Wales to turning it from a barbaric society, as he saw it, into a civilisation. He largely succeeded.

Two decades after the arrival of Governor Phillip and the First Fleet of convicts and their keepers, Macquarie, on his arrival, found Sydney still a primitive town. Twelve years later, in 1822, he sailed home and the Sydney Gazette said that Sydney *'saw her benefactor for the last time'*. Sydney, the paper said, was his *'child.'*

Macquarie wanted Australia to be as moral – or more – as England, and clamped down on drinking and gambling by Europeans and Aborigines alike. He opened schools, built hospitals and courthouses and ordered a new town plan for Sydney. He brought emancipists – former convicts – into the community. He built schools for Aborigines and punished white settlers who mistreated them.

Naturally – human nature being what it is – there were those like Samuel Marsden, *'the flogging parson',* and John Macarthur, the man who saw himself above the law, who resented Macquarie's attempts to improve the lives of emancipists and Aborigines, and smarted under his authoritarian manner. They succeeded in having Macquarie recalled, and two years after he left Australia he died, a bitter man. His legacy, however, lives on.

Towards the end of the age of Macquarie a new type of inhabitant had, literally, been born. Visitors from England remarked on the youths of the colony: they were taller and more slender than their British counterparts; they had fairer complexions and, often, great physical strength; and they had no interest in, and were often antagonistic towards, England, the mother country.

They were called Cornstalks or Currency Lads and Lasses but they were Australians, the name first suggested by Matthew Flinders and the name that Macquarie recommended the British Government call the continent.

• PHAR LAP •

The most popular exhibit in any museum in Australia is a stuffed horse: Phar Lap.

He stands 208 centimetres high from the ground to the top of his head – incredibly lifelike – in a glass case at Museum Victoria. Millions have gone to see him since his death seven decades ago.

Why?

For one thing, Phar Lap – the name comes from the Thai word meaning *'lightning'* – was a horse that gave people hope. Like Don Bradman, his contemporary in the Depression years of the early 1930s, Phar Lap was virtually guaranteed to succeed. That meant you could put a *'quid'* on him and be almost guaranteed to win. And that meant you had enough money to pay the rent and the bills and put food on the table for a week or more.

And for another, his death remains one of the great whodunits.

He wasn't always a winner. He was an ungainly colt from New Zealand who did nothing to excite his owner or his public – they didn't exist then – for his first dozen races.

An also-ran, as the racing form guides had it. Then Phar Lap hit his straps. In his next 41 starts Phar Lap won 36 times.

Think about that. It meant that this big horse with his huge stride was virtually unbeatable.

No wonder Phar Lap was revered – and feared. Bookmakers, of course, loathed him. Four months before the 1930 Melbourne Cup two men in a car tried to shoot *'Big Red'*. They might have succeeded but for young Tommy Woodcock, the stable hand who was Phar Lap's closest human companion. Woodcock put himself and the pony he was riding between Phar Lap and the gunmen and the gunshots went wide.

Phar Lap won the 1930 Cup and the following year he was given an impossibly heavy weight to carry. He couldn't win. Jim Pike, Phar Lap's jockey, nursed him home in eighth place. It was to be his last race in Australia – and his second-last race.

In January 1932, two months later, Phar Lap sailed for America to run in the richest race in the world. He was slow to get going and gave the field a start that seemed certain to leave him an also-ran – just like the old days. But he was bigger and better now and he romped home first. America was amazed. Sixteen days later Big Red was dead.

How did he die? Many thought, and still believe, that once again bookmakers wanted Phar Lap dead. He was poisoned, they said. Others put his death down to accidental poisoning. Whatever, he died with his head in Tommy Woodcock's arms. Australia mourned, deeply.

Phar Lap's mighty heart, twice the size of a normal horse's, is in Canberra. His skeleton is in Wellington, and his stuffed hide, a triumph of taxidermy, in Melbourne. Like Ned Kelly, who was hanged just down the road, Phar Lap is now part of the Australian legend.

• EDWARD 'WEARY' • DUNLOP

> PRISONER OF WAR SURGEON

We know all about you and your [wireless] set. You will be executed, but first you will talk.

Edward 'Weary' Dunlop's wrists were manacled behind his back, encircling the trunk of a tree. Facing him were his Japanese interrogator and soldiers with fixed bayonets.

He was not going to talk, the big feller knew that, and in the moments he had to live the past rushed up. He recalled '...*a time at school when for an escapade I anticipated expulsion and disgrace.*' Now, facing an excruciating death, he reflected wryly that the school-days threat of disgrace seemed far worse than the bayoneting he was about to get.

Weary shook off those memories and told his interrogator what he thought of him. He talked so defiantly, so proudly, that the man, admiring the prisoner's courage, relented and ordered him tortured instead.

A champion boxer, a rugby forward for Australia, a pharmacist and surgeon of renown, a pioneer in the fight against cancer, he saved the lives of hundreds of prisoners of war. He was knighted for his services to medicine and given many awards, yet Sir Edward Dunlop's achievements remain largely ignored in the roll call of Australian heroes. In books dedicated to famous Australians and written over the last four decades, his name is often missing from the index.

His citation for an Order of the British Empire read in part: '*This Officer was in command of a force of 850 POWs in Thailand...Regardless of his own safety he constantly opposed all attempts by the Japanese to force sick men to work, and in doing so received a very large amount of severe beatings and punishments. Although seriously ill himself, he displayed amazing skill as surgeon and during an epidemic of cholera he worked long hours continuously with the result of saving many lives [his] name became legendary as the King of the River in all the Railway camps in Burma and amongst all nationalities there.*'

He didn't get the OBE.

Only in 1993, when he died aged 86, did we come to realise what an extraordinary hero had been in our midst.

Weary served with his medical unit in the Middle East, Greece, Crete and Africa before he was captured in Java and spent the next three years on the notorious Burma–Thailand '*Death Railway*'. By nature, said one who knew him, he was '*a gentle man, a dreamer*', but, faced with the appalling conditions in the prisoner of war camp, with thousands of men dying of brutality, starvation and all manner of disease, Weary knew that he had to be a man of action. He himself suffered a horrific variety of illness in the camps, afflicted by malaria, cholera, hepatitis, pneumonia, pellagra, sand fly fever and beriberi among more than a dozen diseases.

Weary also kept up morale through the invaluable wireless set he concealed from the Japanese. '*I'd see these fellers off at the crack of dawn, just carrying their rice for the day, and then they would drag in any time up until midnight, some of them on their hands and knees,*' he recalled. Exhausted, the captives would hear the whispered news that kept them from total despair: the war was being won.

Weary hid the radio parts in the hollow centres of bamboo, in a cholera ward where guards were reluctant to go, or sewn into his cap or his pack. Then there were the secret diary, the compass and the maps. If any one of them had been found Weary would have been beheaded.

After the war, Weary Dunlop taught medicine in India and Southeast Asia and, as President of the Ex-POW Association of Australia, dedicated himself to campaigning for the men and women who had survived the camps.

• SAM ISAACS •

Sam Isaacs, a young Aboriginal stockman, was riding on the beach on 2 December 1875 when he abruptly reined in his horse – out in the turbulent surf, a shipwreck: a steamer wallowing and ready to go down with scores of men and women trapped aboard her.

Sam Isaacs worked for the Bussell family on their property near the mouth of what came to be called Margaret River. At the house 16-year-old Grace Bussell was helping her mother hang Christmas decorations when he burst in. Grace and Sam grabbed some rope and galloped to the scene.

From a cliff top they saw lifeboats being lowered. Twenty passengers of the SS *Georgette* scrambled into the first boat. As it was lowered a wave crashed against its hull, snapping the boat in half and plunging all into the surf. Eight women and children drowned immediately, and another four were soon to drown.

Grace and Sam rode down the cliff face and into the surf. Out beyond the second line of breakers they reached the boat. Then, with women and children clinging to their horses and the trailing ropes, they turned for the shore. Then they went back for more. For four hours they risked their lives. There had been 48 on the boat and 36 lived to tell the tale of Grace and Sam.

The story went around the world and the Royal Humane Society awarded Grace its silver medal for bravery. Sam got a bronze. That's how things were then. In 1897, years later, the government awarded Sam 100 acres of land at Ferndale, near the Bussell homestead.

• HORRIE THE WAR DOG •

He was just a mutt, a little runt of a dog with a big heart beating under his skinny ribs. But Horrie saw action in some of the darkest days of the Second World War (1939–45). In Egypt, he trained with the Australian Infantry Force's 2/1st Australian Machine Gun battalion for the campaigns to come. In Greece, Horrie and his mates were relentlessly strafed and bombed by the invading Germans. In Crete, he was wounded when his ship went down. In Syria, he fought French troops who had gone over to the Germans.

Through it all, Horrie's courage and fighting spirit never deserted him. And he never wavered in his devotion to his mates.

Horrie joined the AIF in Egypt in 1942 when Jim Moody and Don Gill, a couple of Aussie privates stationed in the Western Desert, noticed a pup chasing lizards among the rocks. He was hopping with fleas, half-starved and rather comical looking with stumpy legs, a long body and not much of a tail to wag. But he was clearly in need of a good feed and Jim and Don scooped him up and took him back to the camp.

Within a week, Horrie, as they called him, was everybody's mate, and a valued member of the battalion. No route march could start until Horrie was at the front. The little dog took his place at the head of the column and proudly led it out. At night he guarded the camp. But then it was time for action.

The days of training and route marches were over, and the battalion was ordered to Greece to help stem the German invasion. Horrie went too. It was against regulations, but by now he had been trained to travel, keeping still and quiet in Jim's kitbag.

Horrie and his mates arrived in Athens, but straight away the Germans were diving-bombing and machine-gunning them. The Allies began what was to become one of the most disastrous retreats of the war. Day after day, the columns, exposed on the road, were attacked from the air. Horrie became an air-raid siren – better than any operated by human observers.

With a dog's superior hearing, Horrie knew when the German bombers were coming. Immediately, he would start a frenzied, angry barking. It was the signal for men to dive for cover and by the time the planes roared overhead they had been able to get some protection.

Horrie and his mates then went to Crete. There they came under attack from German bombers once again. Horrie was hit – shrapnel from a bomb pierced his shoulder.

Horrie never whimpered when they dug it out. But that was it for Horrie. Jim Moody smuggled the little dog onto a homeward-bound ship that took him to Jim's parents' in Melbourne. Jim went off to fight in New Guinea knowing that Horrie would miss his mates, but wouldn't be short of a cuddle and a good feed.

When the war was over, the stories began to come out – one of them Horrie's. Officials heard about the dog that had come all the way from Egypt. Had he evaded quarantine regulations? Jim owned up. He thought nothing would come of it.

Jim was wrong.

Horrie, the little mongrel dog who had become a legend with the troops, was ordered to be put down – destroyed by a heartless bureaucracy. Around Australia, men and women who knew of Horrie and loved him shed tears.

Horrie's memory lives on in an exhibit at the Australian War Memorial in Canberra. There, to remind us of the plucky little mongrel, is the ventilated rucksack he travelled in, the little coat he wore, and his campaign medals.

Horrie the War Dog's execution shocked a nation and became part of our folklore. A brave little dog, a hero to thousands of servicemen who had fought alongside him, *'destroyed'* by the hands of vicious and petty officials. That is what we believed for six decades and that is why for many years wreaths were laid in his honour on Anzac Day.

But did Horrie really die? The truth is that Horrie lived to fight and play another day. *'He was whisked away to northern Victoria, where he lived out his days and sired many puppies,'* Anthony Hill revealed in his book on animals who served with Australian forces, *Animal Heroes* (Penguin, 2005).

Jim had found a dog in the local pound. The dog looked like Horrie and no one wanted him. He was about to be put down. Jim took him out of the pound and gave him to the officials. It saddened Jim Moodie, but the substitute dog was doomed in any case. He died, but Horrie was spared.

• MARK ELLA •

On Saturdays, Mark Ella recalled, *'Mum would say, "Here's your breakfast and I'll see you at dinner time."'*

Mark Ella came from the humblest of beginnings: a small, very crowded house in La Perouse, Sydney. He had 11 brothers and sisters. But he also had a very strong, loving family.

After breakfast, he said, *'We'd wander around, maybe get a couple of bucks for caddying at New South Wales Golf Club, go diving for the 20-cent pieces the tourists would throw us young Aboriginal kids at the Bear Island wharf – we were like circus animals I guess, performing for them, I guess, but we didn't care – and then in the afternoon we'd play footie in the street again. During the week we'd play pretty much every afternoon. Lots and lots of footie.'*

Mark Ella went on playing lots and lots of footie until he stunned the rugby world by announcing his retirement. His international career spanned only six years, from 1979 to 1984, and he was just 25, the same number of Test caps he won. But on his retirement he was acknowledged as one of the greatest rugby players of all time. The brilliant David Campese, his fellow Wallaby, and Wally Lewis, the rugby league immortal, called him the best they had played with or against. His Wallabies coach, Bob Dwyer, named him among the five most accomplished Australian players he had seen and said he was number one for *'mastery of the game's structure'*. Others think he was simply the best rugby fly half/five-eighth of all time.

What isn't in dispute is the way Mark Ella's exceptional ball-handling skills, his straight running and his ability to keep the ball alive virtually re-invented the game.

Ella's unique brand of rugby ignited an unprecedented golden period for Australia and thrilled spectators around the world. In turn he was awarded captaincy of the Wallabies and became the first Indigenous Young Australian of the Year in 1983, and was awarded the Order of Australia in 1984.

Mark Ella was particularly admired in England, France, Ireland, Scotland and Wales. The London Times sports writer Frank Keating wrote: *'If some destructive process were to eliminate all we know about rugby, only Ella surviving, we could reconstruct from him, from his way of playing and living rugby and from the man himself, every outline of the game, every essential character and its flavour which have contributed to rugby, the form of it and its soul, and its power to inspire.'*

• JOHN LANDY •

The great sports fantasy of the 20th century was that it was possible for a man to run a mile in under four minutes. Realistically, however, the experts agreed it couldn't be done. Mile runners could get close, but it was simply physically impossible. Some experts thought that you could die trying.

But in the early 1950s Roger Bannister in England and John Landy in Australia – a modest but intense young man, the pride of the nation – were running the fastest miles ever, week in week out, edging ever closer to the magic four-minute mark.

The question the world was now asking was not would they die in the attempt, but which of them would go under four minutes first? On 6 May 1954 Roger Bannister crossed the line in three minutes, 59.4 seconds. Forty-six days later in Finland John Landy ran a three minutes, 58 seconds – almost two seconds faster than Bannister's time.

Immediately the focus shifted to the coming Empire (now Commonwealth) Games. Newspapers internationally recognised that the world was about to see a race without precedent. Two men, the only two, ever to do the *'impossible'*, racing against each other in what was quickly, and for once quite correctly, dubbed, *'The Mile of the Century'*.

The media went into a feeding frenzy. This was a sports story the like of which athletics had never known. *'It was like a world title fight,'* Landy recalled. *'It went on for weeks.'* The Mile of the Century was also a milestone in sporting and television history: the first time any sporting event had been televised in the US from coast to coast. A hundred million watched it in North America, a huge audience 60 years ago when only a minority of people had a television set. In England and Australia 50 million sent up prayers.

Both men stepped up to the starting line with strategies based ontheir knowledge of each other. Landy's was simple. He was going to try to run Bannister off his feet.

Landy's plan worked better than he had anticipated up until the halfway mark. He had opened a huge gap, around 15 yards. But then Bannister began to reel him in. With 120 yards to go, and rounding the final bend, Landy looked the 'wrong' way – over his left shoulder – to see where Bannister was. 'When I looked up the other way he was going past my right-hand side and of course the race was all over,' Landy said.

Both men had run sub-four-minute miles, but Bannister had won the Mile of the Century.

Could he have won if he'd looked right, first? 'That's nonsense,' Landy said.

What he didn't say was that he had cut the side of the instep of his right foot two days before the race. A doctor told Landy to forget about running the next day. A Canadian sportswriter discovered Landy's secret when he burst in on him in his room and saw the floor smeared with blood. In return for an interview he agreed to keep the story a secret.

In January 1956, after a long, disillusioned break, John Landy returned to Olympic Park, Melbourne, and ran the second-fastest mile in history, second only to his own record. A few weeks later he was set to try to smash that record in the Australian championships.

There were 20,000 at Olympic Park when, in the third lap, the 19-year-old unknown Ron Clarke, caught in the hurly burly as the field bustled to go into the last 440 yards, clipped another's heels and sprawled to the ground. Landy, running behind for one of the few times in his career and trying to hurdle him, caught his spikes on Clarke's arm.

Landy stopped dead and bent down to see if Clarke was injured. Clarke said he was fine, jumped to his feet and rushed to rejoin the race. Landy, sprinting hard, took after him. He had given the lead runner seven seconds and 40 yards, but by the time they reached the turn he was just 15 yards adrift and into the back straight he was within five. He won by 12 yards. His time was four minutes, 4.2 seconds.

The race, and the moment when Landy stopped and bent over the fallen Ron Clarke, is commemorated in a statue at the Melbourne Cricket Ground.

• ICONS •

Well over a hundred years ago a wicket bail was burnt to symbolise the death of English cricket at the hands of the Aussies. The result of this, the Ashes – has become one of our most well-known icons.

Australia's first official game of cricket was played in 1826. Although the first Australian touring team, composed of Aborigines, entertained crowds with boomerang throwing and running backwards, they nevertheless had a successful season in Britain in 1868, foretelling an Australian tradition.

The most notable victory for the Australians was several years later, in 1882, with Billy Murdoch's team becoming the first to defeat England on English home turf. Australia's seven-run victory at The Oval led to the appearance of a death notice, now famous, in the *Sporting Times* of London.

It read:

In affectionate memory of English Cricket which died at The Oval, 29th August, 1882. Deeply lamented by a large circle of sorrowing friends and acquaintances. R.I.P. N.B.. – The body will be cremated and the ashes taken to Australia.

The following year the urn, containing the ashes of a burned cricket stump, was won back by the English. The Ashes now have a permanent home in the Members' Pavilion at Lord's, and while the Ashes no longer reside in our country, Australians justifiably claim the Ashes as an icon of our glorious sporting achievements.

THE ASHES

• ICONS •

The Sydney Harbour Bridge has graced Sydney Harbour since 1932, when it was opened to the public by the Premier of New South Wales, J.T. Lang. The idea of a single arch bridge, running from Dawes Point on the southern shore to Milson's Point on the northern shore, was first proposed by Francis Greenaway, a convict architect, in 1815. Others suggested a floating bridge. In 1888 a Royal commission was appointed to examine a number of different proposals, and the final recommendation from the commission called for a high-level, preferably single-span bridge.

Tenders for the bridge were called for in 1900 but further progress was not made until 1922, when new legislation was passed. New tenders were invited in 1923 and by 1926 the bridge's construction by constructional engineers Dorman Long and Co. (following the design of Dr. J. Bradfield) was finally underway.

In February 1932 the completed Sydney Harbour Bridge was put to the test. Dr Bradfield loaded the bridge with 96 railway engines (weighing the equivalent of 5900 average cars) so the engineers could measure the bridge's performance. Given that the bridge would only be able to fit a maximum of 850 cars, parked bumper to bumper, this test was rather excessive. But it proved to the population that the bridge was a sturdy one.

The Sydney Harbour Bridge is Australia's largest bridge (although not the longest – this feat belongs to the West Gate Bridge), and is the second longest single-span bridge in the world. It was originally intended that the bridge would be the world's longest steel span, but four months prior to its opening, a similarly designed bridge, just 635 millimetres longer, had opened in New York.

The total weight of the Sydney Harbour Bridge is a massive 52,732 tonnes, with its main span 503 metres long and 49 metres wide. Its total length is 1149 metres.

The deck was designed to accommodate both rail and tram tracks, as well as having roadway and two footways. In 1959 the two eastern tram lanes were converted to roadways.

Some interesting trivia for the fact collectors: the largest rivet used in the construction of the bridge was 39 centimetres long and weighs a hefty 3½ kilograms; six million rivets were used in total; and the longest hanger supporting the deck is 59 metres long and weighs 33 tonnes.

The total capital cost of the distinctly Australian icon was around six million pounds and given its usefulness to Sydneysiders and its recognition as a great Australian icon, it was worth every penny.

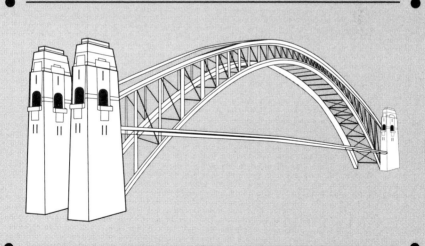

QUOTES

• QUOTES •

> CONTENTS <

• A •

ABILITY

The art of getting credit for all the
home runs somebody else hits.

Casey Stengel

ABSURDITY

A statement of belief manifestly
inconsistent with one's own opinion.

Ambrose Bierce

ACTORS

People who should be
treated like cattle.

Alfred Hitchcock

★ ★ ★

A guy who,
if you ain't talking about him,
ain't listening.

Marlon Brando

> ALCOHOLIC <

Anyone you don't like
who drinks more than you do.

Dylan Thomas

> APOLOGISE <

To lay the foundation
for a future offense.

Ambrose Bierce

> AUTOBIOGRAPHY <

An obituary in serial form
with the last instalment missing.

Quentin Crisp

★ ★ ★

An unrivalled vehicle for telling
the truth about other people.

Philip Guedalla

★ ★ ★

Something only to be trusted
when it reveals something disgraceful.

George Orwell

· B ·

BABY

A misshapen creature
of no particular age, sex or condition,
chiefly remarkable for the violence
of the sympathies and antipathies
it excites in others.

Ambrose Bierce

★ ★ ★

A loud noise at one end
and no sense of responsibility
at the other.

Ronald Knox

BARRISTER

A word in the dictionary that
comes between bankrupt and bastard.

Anon

> BIMBO <

A woman who's
not pretty enough to be a model,
not smart enough to be an actress,
and not nice enough to be
a poisonous snake.

P. J. O'Rourke

> BORE <

A person who talks
when you wish him to listen.

Ambrose Bierce

A man who, when you ask
him how he is, tells you.

Bert Leston Taylor

A person who deprives you of solitude
without providing you with company.

Gian Vincenzo Lavina

• C •

CAT

A soft, indestructible automaton
provided by nature
to be kicked when things go wrong
in the domestic circle.

Ambrose Bierce

An animal
which if crossed with man
would improve man,
but would deteriorate itself.

Mark Twain

CELEBRITY

One who is known by many people
he is glad he doesn't know.

H. L. Mencken

CHILDHOOD

The period of human life
intermediate between the idiocy
of infancy and the folly of youth –
two removes from the sin of manhood
and three from the remorse of age.

Ambrose Bierce

★ ★ ★

A series of happy delusions.

Sydney Smith

 CIVILISATION

A concerted effort to remedy the
blunders and check the practical joking of God.

H. L. Mencken

★ ★ ★

The lamb's skin
in which barbarism
masquerades.

T. B. Aldrich

★ ★ ★

Something that reaches no lower than
our clothes. Humanity is still essentially
Yahoo-manity.

W. R. Inge

• D •

DEATH

A wonderful way of cutting down
on your expenses.

Woody Allen

★ ★ ★

The only thing society
hasn't succeeded in
completely vulgarising.

Aldous Huxley

★ ★ ★

What some patients do merely
to humiliate the doctor.

Voltaire

DELUSION

The father of a most respectable family,
comprising Enthusiasm, Affection,
Self-denial, Faith, Hope, Charity
and many other goodly
sons and daughters.

Ambrose Bierce

> DEPRESSION <

The state of mind produced by a
newspaper joke, a minstrel performance,
or the contemplation of another's success.

Ambrose Bierce

> DIVORCE <

Future tense of marry.

Anon

From the Latin word
meaning to rip out a man's genitals
through his wallet.

Robin Williams

> DRAMA <

Life with the dull bits cut out.

Alfred Hitchcock

> DRUGS <

Something that has taught an
entire generation of American kids
the metric system.

P. J. O'Rourke

· E ·

> EDIBLE <

Good to eat and wholesome to digest,
as a worm to a toad, a toad to a snake,
a snake to a pig, a pig to a man,
and a man to a worm.

Ambrose Bierce

> EGOTISM <

The anesthetic that
dulls the pains of stupidity.

Frank Leahy

> EMAIL <

A useful device for gossiping
with friends when you're in the office –
and still looking busy.

Anon

A means of communicating
with people you don't want to talk to.

Anon

THE ENGLISH

A race of cold-blooded queers with nasty
complexions and terrible teeth who once
conquered half the world, but still
haven't figured out central heating.

P. J. O'Rourke

EXPERIENCE

The name everyone gives
to their mistakes.

Oscar Wilde

A comb which nature gives to men
when they are bald.

Eastern proverb

The wisdom that enables us to recognize
as an undesirable old acquaintance
the folly that we have already embraced.

Ambrose Bierce

A series of failures.

H. L. Mencken

• F •

⟩ FAITH ⟨

An illogical belief in the occurrence
of the improbable.

H. L. Mencken

Belief without evidence in what is told
by one who speaks without knowledge
of things without parallel.

Ambrose Bierce

⟩ FAMILY ⟨

A unit composed not only of children
but of men, women, an occasional
animal, and the common cold.

Ogden Nash

⟩ FASHION ⟨

A form of ugliness so intolerable,
we have to alter it every six months.

Oscar Wilde

FEMINISM

The belief that women
should have the opportunity
to behave as badly as men.

Anon

FLATTERY

A bit like a cigarette –
all right as long as you
don't inhale.

Adlai Stevenson

FOOL

Someone who doesn't share
your political beliefs.

Anon

THE FUTURE

That period of time
in which our affairs prosper,
our friends are true and
our happiness is assured.

Ambrose Bierce

· G ·

GAMBLING

The sure way of getting
nothing for something.

Wilson Mizner

GESTICULATION

Any movement made by a foreigner.

J. B. Morton

GOLF

A good walk spoiled.

Mark Twain

A game whose aim is to hit
a very small ball into an even
smaller hole, with weapons singularly
ill-designed for the purpose.

Winston Churchill

GOOD BREEDING

Concealing how much we think
of ourselves and how little
we think of the other person.

Mark Twain

GOOD INTENTIONS

What the way to Hell is paved with.

Proverb

GOOD LOSER

A loser.

Paul Newman

GRIEVANCE

Something which supplies a purpose in life.

Eric Hoffer

GUILT

The condition of one who is known to
have committed an indiscretion,
as distinguished from the state of mind
of him who has covered his tracks.

Ambrose Bierce

• H •

 HANGOVER

When the brew of the night
meets the dark of the day.

Brendan Behan

★ ★ ★

The wrath of grapes.

Geoffrey Barnard

 HAPPINESS

An agreeable sensation
arising from contemplating
the misery of another.

Ambrose Bierce

★ ★ ★

Nothing more than health,
and a poor memory.

Albert Schweitzer

 HEDGEHOG

The cactus of the animal kingdom.

Ambrose Bierce

HEREDITY

What sets the parents of a teenager
wondering about each other.

Laurence Peter

HISTORIAN

An unsuccessful novelist.

H. L. Mencken

A broad-gauge gossip.

Ambrose Bierce

HOME

The place of last resort – open all night.

Ambrose Bierce

HYPOCHONDRIAC

Someone who enjoys bad health.

Anon

HYPOCRISY

The homage paid by vice to virtue.

Duc de la Rochefoucauld

IDEAS

One of the greatest pains
to human nature.

Walter Bageshot

IMMORALITY

The morality of those who are
having a better time.

H. L. Mencken

INFLATION

Prosperity with high blood pressure.

Arnold Glasgow

When prices go from
reasonable to expensive to
'How much have you got with you?'

Bob Hope

INSANITY

A perfectly rational adjustment
to an insane world.

R. D. Laing

IRELAND

The only country in the world
where you can get drunk
and not wake up
with a guilty conscience.

John Huston

The only place in the world
where procrastination
takes on a sense of urgency.

Dave Allen

IVORY

A substance
kindly provided by nature
for making billiard balls.
It is usually harvested from
the mouths of elephants.

Ambrose Bierce

· J ·

THE JAPANESE

People who have
perfected good manners
and made them indistinguishable
from rudeness.

Paul Theroux

JEALOUSY

The theory that some fellow
has just as little taste.

H. L. Mencken

The dragon that slays love
under the pretence
of keeping it alive.

Havelock Ellis

JEWS

A race of people just like
everyone else, only more so.

Arnold Foster

JUDGE

An officer appointed to mislead,
restrain, hypnotize, cajole, seduce,
browbeat, flabbergast and bamboozle
a jury in such a manner
that it will forget all the facts and
give its decision to the best lawyer.

H. L. Mencken

A person who is always interfering
in disputes in which he has
no personal interest.

Ambrose Bierce

JUDGEMENT DAY

God's audit.

Hal Roach

JUSTICE

A commodity which
in a more or less adulterated condition
the State sells to the citizen
as a reward for his allegiance, taxes
and personal service.

Ambrose Bierce

· K ·

> KANGAROO <

An unconventional kind of animal
which in shape is farther than any other
from being the square of its base.
It is assisted in jumping by its tail
(which makes very good soup).

Ambrose Bierce

> KARATE <

A form of martial arts
in which people who have had
years of training can, using only
their hands and feet,
make some of the worst movies
in the history of the world.

Dave Barry

> KILL <

To create a vacancy
without nominating a successor.

Ambrose Bierce

KILT

A costume sometimes worn
by Scotchmen in America and
Americans in Scotland.

Ambrose Bierce

KINDNESS

A brief preface to
ten volumes of exaction.

Ambrose Bierce

KING

A male person
commonly known in America
as a *'crowned head'*, although
he never wears a crown and
has usually no head to speak of.

Ambrose Bierce

KISS

A word invented by poets
to rhyme for *'bliss'*.

Ambrose Bierce

• L •

LADY

One who
never shows her underwear
unintentionally.

Lillian Day

★ ★ ★

A vulgarian word
for a woman.

Ambrose Bierce

★ ★ ★

A word
most often used to describe
someone you wouldn't want to talk to
for even five minutes.

Fran Lebowitz

LIAR

A lawyer with a roving commission.

Ambrose Bierce

LICKSPITTLE

A useful functionary,
not infrequently found
editing a newspaper.

Ambrose Bierce

LIFE

Anything that dies
when you stomp on it.

Dave Barry

A maze in which
we take the wrong turning
before we have learned to walk.

Cyril Connolly

A spiritual pickle
preserving the body from decay.

Ambrose Bierce

A sexually transmitted disease –
and the mortality rate
is 100 per cent.

R. D. Laing

#

 MAD

Affected with a high degree
of intellectual independence.

Ambrose Bierce

 MARRIAGE

A bribe to make a housekeeper
think she's a householder.

Thornton Wilder

★ ★ ★

An institution which is popular because
it combines the minimum of temptation
with the maximum of opportunity.

George Bernard Shaw

★ ★ ★

A licence for two people
to insult each other.

Brendan Behan

★ ★ ★

A sort of friendship recognised by the police.

Robert Louis Stevenson

MASTURBATION

Sex with someone you love.

Woody Allen

MEALTIME

The only time in the day
when children resolutely
refuse to eat.

Fran Lebowitz

THE MEANING OF LIFE

That it stops.

Franz Kafka

MISFORTUNE

The kind of fortune
that never misses.

Ambrose Bierce

MURDER

Always a mistake:
one should never do anything
that one cannot talk about
after dinner.

Oscar Wilde

• N •

NATION

A society united by a delusion about
its ancestry and by a common hatred
of its neighbors.

William R. Inge

NEUROTICS

Those who founded our religions
and created our masterpieces.

Marcel Proust

NATURAL DEATH

Where you die by yourself without the aid of a doctor.

Mark Twain

NEIGHBOUR

One whom we are commanded to love
as ourselves, and who does all he knows
how to make us disobedient.

Ambrose Bierce

NEW ZEALAND

A country of thirty million sheep, three million
of whom think they're human.

Barry Humphries

Land of the long white shroud.

Anon

Where men are men, and sheep feel nervous.

Graffiti

NEWLYWED

A guy who tells his wife
when he gets a pay rise.

Leonard Louis Levinson

NEWS

What a chap who doesn't care
much about anything wants to read.

Evelyn Waugh

NOUVELLE CUISINE

Nothing on your plate and plenty on your bill.

Paul Bocuse

OBSCENITY

Whatever happens to shock some
elderly and ignorant magistrate.

Bertrand Russell

OPPORTUNIST

A person who strikes a 50-50 deal
in such a way that he insists on
getting the hyphen as well.

Jack Benny

OPTIMISM

A kind of heart stimulant –
the digitalis of failure.

Elbert Hubbard

The doctrine of belief that everything
is beautiful, including what is ugly,
everything good, especially the bad,
and everything right that is wrong.

Ambrose Bierce

OSTEOPATH

One who argues that all human
ills are caused by the pressure of
hard bone upon soft tissue.
The proof of his theory is to be found
in the heads of those who believe it.

H. L. Mencken

OUT OF DOORS

What you must pass through in order to
get from your apartment to a taxi-cab.

Fran Lebowitz

That part of one's environment
upon which no government
has been able to collect taxes.
Chiefly useful to inspire poets.

Ambrose Bierce

OYSTER

A slimy, gobby shellfish
which civilization gives men
the hardihood to eat
without removing its entrails.

Ambrose Bierce

• P •

> PARENTS <

The bones on which children
sharpen their teeth.

Peter Ustinov

> PARTY <

A roomful of noisy people trying to get
off with or away from other people.

Anon

> PATIENCE <

A minor form of despair,
disguised as a virtue.

Ambrose Bierce

> PEDESTRIANS <

People who are knocked down
by motor cars.

J. B. Morton

PHILOSOPHY

Something that consists largely of
one philosopher arguing that all others
are jackasses. He usually proves it,
and I should add that he also usually
proves that he is one himself.

H. L. Mencken

A route of many roads
leading from nowhere
to nothing.

Ambrose Bierce

What teaches us to bear
with equanimity
the misfortunes
of our neighbours.

Oscar Wilde

PLATONIC RELATIONSHIP

Something that
is only possible between
a husband and wife.

Irving Kristol

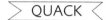

QUACK

A murderer without a licence.

Ambrose Bierce

QUILL

An implement of torture yeilded by a
goose and commonly weilded by an ass.
This use of the quill is now obsolete, but
its modern equivalent, the steel pen, is
wielded by the same everlasting Presence.

Ambrose Bierce

QUOTATION

The act of repeating erroneously
the words of another.
The words erroneously repeated

Ambrose Bierce

• R •

RADICAL

Someone who becomes
a conservative
on the day after the revolution.

Hannah Arendt

A man with both feet
planted firmly in the air.

Franklin D. Roosevelt

RELATIONS

A tedious pack of people
who haven't got the remotest knowledge
of how to live, nor the smallest instinct
about when to die.

Oscar Wilde

People that you call on,
or that call on you, according to
whether they are rich or poor.

Ambrose Bierce

> REMARRIAGE <

The triumph of hope over reason.

Samuel Johnson

> RIOT <

A popular entertainment
given to the military
by innocent bystanders.

Ambrose Bierce

> ROCK AND ROLL <

The sound of grown men
throwing tantrums.

Bono

> ROBBER <

Vulgar name for one
who is successful in obtaining
the property of others.

Ambrose Bierce

> RUSSIA <

The greatest country in the world,
were it not necessary to eat or wear clothes.

Yakov Smirnoff

• S •

THE SCOTS

Sour, stingy, depressing beggars
who parade around in schoolgirl's skirts
with nothing on underneath.

P. J. O'Rourke

SECRET

Something that three may keep,
if two of them are dead.

Benjamin Franklin

SEX

One of the nine reasons
for reincarnation.
The other eight are unimportant.

Henry Miller

The most fun you can have
without laughing.

Woody Allen

SKIING

Wearing three thousand dollars' worth
of clothes and equipment and driving
two hundred miles in the snow
in order to stand around at
a bar and get drunk.

P. J. O'Rourke

★ ★ ★

An activity that combines outdoor fun with
knocking down trees with your face.

Dave Barry

SLEEP

Death without the responsibility.

Fran Lebowitz

SPORT

War minus the shooting.

George Orwell

SUICIDE

Cheating the doctors out of a job.

Josh Billings

• T •

TEA

Something to amuse the idle,
relax the studious and dilute
the full meals of those
who cannot use exercise and
will not use abstinence.

Samuel Johnson

TEACHING

The last refuge of feeble minds
with a classical education.

Aldous Huxley

TEENAGERS

God's punishment for having sex.

Anon

THINKING

The hardest work there is, which is
probably why so few engage in it.

Henry Ford

TIME

The surest poison.

Ralph Waldo Emerson

TOLERANCE

The virtue of a man
without convictions.

G. K. Chesterton

TREE

A tall vegetable intended by nature
to serve as a penal apparatus.

Ambrose Bierce

TRUTH

Something that is never pure,
and rarely simple.

Oscar Wilde

TRUTHFUL

Dumb and illiterate.

Ambrose Bierce

· U ·

ULTIMATUM

In diplomacy,
a last demand before
resorting to concessions.

Ambrose Bierce

UN-AMERICAN

Wicked, intolerable, heathenish.

Ambrose Bierce

UNIVERSITY

A place for elevating sons
above the social rank
of their fathers.

H. L. Mencken

• V •

VENICE

Like eating a whole box
of chocolate liqueurs
in one go.

Truman Capote

VICE

It's own reward

Quentin Crisp

VIOLENCE

The repartee
of the illiterate.

Alan Brien

VIRTUE

The avoidance of vices
that do not attract us.

Robert Lynd

VIRTUES

Certain abstentions.

Ambrose Bierce

VISITORS

Like fish,
they begin to stink after three days.

Anon

VULGARITY

The rich man's
modest contribution
to democracy.

Samuel Johnson

The garlic
in the salad of taste.

Cyril Connolly

• W •

WEDDING

A funeral where you can smell your own flowers.

Eddie Cantor

★ ★ ★

A ceremony at which
two persons undertake to become one,
one undertakes to become nothing, and
nothing undertakes to become supportable.

Ambrose Bierce

★ ★ ★

A device for exciting envy in women and terror in men.

H. L. Mencken

WHISKY

The most popular of the cold cures that don't work.

Leonard Rossiter

WIFE

A woman who turns an old rake
into a lawn-mower.

Jack Benny

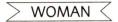 **WOMAN**

God's second mistake.

Friedrich Nietzsche

 ★ ★ ★

A foe to friendship,
an inescapable punishment,
a necessary evil.

John Chrysostom

 ★ ★ ★

An animal usually living in the vicinity
of Man, and having a rudimentary
susceptibility to domestication.

Ambrose Bierce

 ★ ★ ★

Before marriage an agente
provocateuse: After marriage,
a gendarme.

H. L. Mencken

 WORK

The refuge of those
who have nothing better to do.

Oscar Wilde

· X · Y · Z ·

> XENOPHOBIA <

The resentment of the fact
that most people in the world
are foreigners.

Anon

> XMAS <

Popular festival made to sound
like a skin disease.

Mike Barfield

> YACHT CLUB <

An asylum for landsmen
who would rather die of drink
than be seasick.

H. L. Mencken

> YEAR <

A period of three hundred
and sixty-five disappointments.

Ambrose Bierce

> YOUTH <

A disease that must
be borne with patiently!
Time, indeed will cure it.

R. H. Benson

Something very new; twenty years ago
no one mentioned it.

Coco Chanel

> ZEAL <

A nervous disorder afflicting
the young and inexperienced.

Ambrose Bierce

> ZOO <

A place for animals to study the habits
of human beings.

Oliver Hurford

• ICONS •

Although the Eureka flag now rests in a Ballarat museum, it once flew in the nearby goldfields in arguably the most famous 15 minutes in Australian history. The year was 1854, and tension on the Ballarat goldfields had been mounting for some time. The diggers were resentful of Governor Hotham: every digger had no choice but to pay 30 shillings a month for the right to mine, which was more than the average monthly earnings at that time. To make matters worse, these fees were often collected by the troopers in a brutal manner.

The diggers' anger culminated when, in 1854, the owner of the Eureka Hotel in Ballarat was let off on a charge of murdering a digger. In protest, the hotel was burned to the ground.

After a time the diggers held a meeting at Baker Hill, above Ballarat, where a bonfire was made. Under their own flag they burned their mining licences and elected Peter Lalor, an engineer from Britain, as their leader, and revolutionary Raffaelo Carboni as his deputy.

The men voted to make their stand at Eureka Lead, where they built a stockade and created their Southern Cross flag, also known as the Eureka flag. When the 300 or so troopers finally attacked, there were only around 150 diggers still remaining at the stockade. The troopers ordered the diggers to surrender, and when they refused, the troops charged. The short-lived battle, lasting just 15 minutes, left two dozen diggers dead and double that injured. The rest were imprisoned.

The diggers' stand brought about the elimination of the licence fee. Minders from then on were required to pay only one pound a year for the right to dig for gold and the right to vote. Eureka!

• ICONS •

The Granny Smith apple, green and crisp, is one of the most popular of all apple varieties. Its name comes from Maria Ann Smith, who came to Australia from England in the late 1830s. Here, in the Sydney suburb of Eastwood, Maria grew and sold produce to help with the family income.

The exact origin of the Granny Smith apple remains unknown, with various reports circulating. Once account claims that Maria brought back cases of fruit from the market, in which a few rotting Tasmanian apples were found. Maria reputedly threw these apples out by a nearby creek, where the seeds grew into the first Granny Smith apple trees. Another version has it that Maria threw the peelings and cores of some Tasmanian crab-apples into her garden, the seeds of which germinated into Granny Smiths. And yet another theory espouses that Maria planted some seeds that she found rotting in a gin barrel, and these grew into Granny Smith apple trees.

The truth may never be known, but however the fruit came into being, they now grow around the world and enjoyed all over as a cooking and eating apple.

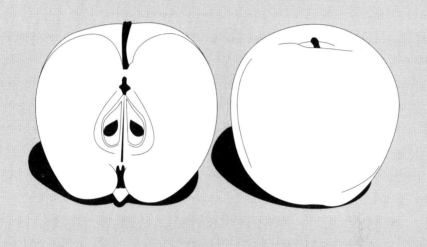

◆ STORIES ◆

• STORIES •

CONTENTS

◆ THE LOADED DOG ◆

―――――― HENRY LAWSON ――――――

Dave Regan, Jim Bently and Andy Page were sinking a shaft at Stony Creek in search of a rich gold quartz reef which was supposed to exist in the vicinity. There is always a rich quartz reef supposed to exist in the vicinity; the only questions are whether it is ten feet or hundreds beneath the surface, and in which direction. They had struck some pretty solid rock, also water which kept them baling. They used the old-fashioned blasting powder and time-fuse; they'd dip the cartridge in melted tallow to make it watertight, get the drill hole as dry as possible, drop in the cartridge with some dry dust, and wad and ram with stiff clay and broken brick. Then they'd light the fuse and get out of the hole and wait. The result was usually an ugly pot-hole in the bottom of the shaft and half a barrow-load of broken rock.

There was plenty of fish in the creek, fresh-water bream, cod, cat-fish, and tailers. The party were fond of fish, and Andy and Dave of fishing. Andy would fish for three hours at a stretch if encouraged by a 'nibble' or a 'bite' now and then – say once in twenty minutes. The butcher was always willing to give meat in exchange for fish when they caught more than they could eat; but now it was winter, and these fish wouldn't bite. However, the creek was low, just a chain of muddy waterholes, from the hole with a few bucketfuls in it to the sizable pool with an average depth of six or seven feet, and they could get fish by bailing out the smaller holes or muddying up the water in the larger ones till the fish rose to the surface. There was the cat-fish, with spikes growing out of the sides of its head, and if you got pricked you'd know it, as Dave said. Andy took off his boots, tucked up his trousers, and went into a hole one day to stir up the mud with his feet, and he knew it. Dave scooped one out with his hand and got pricked, and he knew it too; his arm swelled, and the pain throbbed up into his shoulder, and down into his stomach too, he said, like a toothache he had once, and kept him awake for two nights – only the toothache pain had a 'burred edge', Dave said.

Dave got an idea. *'Why not blow up the fish in the big waterhole with a cartridge?'* he said. *'I'll try it.'*

He thought the thing out and Andy Page worked it out. Andy usually put Dave's theories into practice if they were practicable, or bore the blame for the failure and chaffing of his mates if they weren't.

He made a cartridge about three times the size of those they used in the rock. Jim Bently said it was big enough to blow the bottom out of the river. The inner skin was of stout calico; Andy stuck the end of a six-foot piece of fuse well down in the powder and bound the mouth of the bag firmly to it with whipcord. The idea was to sink the cartridge in the water with the open end of the fuse attached to a float on the surface, ready for lighting. Andy dipped the cartridge in melted beeswax to make it watertight. *'We'll have to leave it some time before we light it,'* said Dave, *'to give the fish time to get over their scare when we put it in, and come nosing around again; so we'll want it watertight.'*

Round the cartridge Andy, at Dave's suggestion, bound a strip of sail canvas – that they had used for making waterbags – to increase the force of the explosion, and round that he pasted layers of stiff brown paper – on the plan of the sort of fireworks we called *'gun-crackers'*. He let the paper dry in the sun, then he sewed a covering of two thicknesses of canvas over it, and bound the thing from end to end with stout fishing line. Dave's schemes were elaborate, and he often worked his inventions out to nothing. The cartridge was rigid and solid enough now – a formidable bomb; but Andy and Dave wanted to be sure. Andy sewed on another layer of canvas, dipped the cartridge in melted tallow, twisted a length of fencing-wire round it as an afterthought, dipped in it tallow again, and stood it carefully against a tent peg, where he'd know where to find it, and wound the fuse loosely round it. Then he went to the campfire to try some potatoes which were boiling in their jackets in a billy, and to see about frying some chops for dinner. Dave and Jim were at work in the claim that morning.

They had a big black young retriever dog – or rather an overgrown pup, a big, foolish, four-footed mate, who was always slobbering round them and lashing their legs with his heavy tail that swung round like a stock whip. Most of his head was usually a red, idiotic slobbering grin of appreciation of his own silliness. He seemed to take life, the world, his two-legged mates, and his own instinct as a huge joke. He'd retrieve anything; he carted back most of the camp rubbish that Andy threw away. They had a cat that died in hot weather, and Andy threw it a good distance away in the scrub; and early one morning the dog found the cat, after it had been dead a week or so, and carried it back to camp, and laid it just inside the tent flaps, where it could make its presence felt when the mates should rise and begin to sniff suspiciously in the sickly smothering atmosphere of the summer sunrise. He used to retrieve them when they went in swimming; he'd jump in after them, and scratch their naked bodies with his paws. They loved him for his good-heartedness and his foolishness, but when they wished to enjoy a swim they had to tie him up in camp.

He watched Andy with great interest all morning making the cartridge, and hindered him considerably, trying to help; but about noon he went off to the claim to see how Dave and Jim were getting on, and to come home to dinner with them. Andy saw them coming, and put a panful of mutton chops on the fire. Andy was cook today;

Dave and Jim stood with their backs to the fire, as bushmen do in all weathers, waiting till dinner should be ready. The retriever went nosing round after something he seemed to have missed.

Andy's brain still worked on the cartridge; his eye was caught by the glare of an empty kerosene tin lying in the bushes, and it struck him that it wouldn't be a bad idea to sink the cartridge packed with clay, sand, or stones in the tin, to increase the force of the explosion. He may have been all out, from a scientific point of view, but the notion looked all right to him. Jim Bently, by the way, wasn't interested in their 'damned silliness'. Andy noticed an empty treacle tin – the sort with the little tin neck or spout soldered on to the top for the convenience of pouring out the treacle – and it struck him that this would have made the best kind of cartridge-case: he would only have had to pour in the powder, stick the fuse through the neck, and cork and seal it with beeswax. He was turning to suggest this to Dave, when Dave glanced over his shoulder to see how the chops were doing – and bolted. He explained afterwards that he thought he heard the pan spluttering extra, and looked to see if the chops were burning. Jim Bently looked behind and bolted after Dave. Andy stood stock-still, staring after them.

'Run, Andy! Run!' they shouted back at him. *Run! Look behind you, you fool!* Andy turned slowly and looked, and there, close behind him, was the retriever with the cartridge in his mouth – wedged into the broadest and silliest grin. And that wasn't all. The dog had come round the fire to Andy, and the loose end of the fuse had trailed and waggled over the burning sticks into the blaze; Andy had slit and nicked the firing end to the fuse well, and now it was hissing and spitting properly.

Andy's legs started with a jolt; his legs started before his brain did, and he made after Dave and Jim. And the dog followed Andy.

Dave and Jim were good runners – Jim the best – for a short distance; Andy was slow and heavy, but he had the strength and the wind and could last. The dog capered round him, delighted as a dog could be to find his mates, as he thought, on for a frolic. Dave and Jim kept shouting back, *'Don't foller us! Don't foller us, you coloured fool!'* But Andy kept on, no matter how they dodged. They could never explain, any more than the dog, why they followed each other, but so they ran, Dave keeping in Jim's track in all its turnings, Andy after Dave, and the dog circling round Andy – the live fuse swishing in all directions and hissing and spluttering and stinking. Jim yelling at Dave not to follow him. Dave shouting to Andy to go in another direction – to *'spread out'*, and Andy roaring at the dog to go home. Then Andy's brain began to work, stimulated by the crisis; he tried to get a running kick at the dog, but the dog dodged; he snatched up sticks and stones and threw them at the dog and ran on again. The retriever saw that he'd made a mistake about Andy, and left him and bounded after Dave. Dave, who had the presence of mind to think that the fuse's time wasn't up yet, made a dive and a grab for the dog, caught him by the tail, and as he swung round snatched the cartridge out of his mouth and flung it as far as he could; the dog immediately bounded after it and retrieved it. Dave roared and cursed at the dog, who, seeing that Dave was offended, left him and went after Jim, who was well ahead. Jim swung to a sapling and went up it like a native bear; it was a young sapling, and Jim couldn't safely get more than ten or twelve feet from the ground. The dog laid the cartridge, as carefully as it were a kitten, at the foot of the sapling, and capered and leaped and whooped joyously round under Jim. The big pup reckoned that this was part of the lark – he was all right now – it was Jim who was out for a spree. The fuse sounded as if it were going a mile a minute. Jim tried to climb higher and the sapling bent and cracked. Jim fell on his feet and ran. The dog swooped on the cartridge and followed. It all took but a very few moments. Jim ran to a digger's hole, about ten feet deep, and dropped down into it – landing on soft mud – and was safe. The dog grinned sardonically down on him, over the edge, for a moment, as if he thought it would be a good lark to drop the cartridge down on Jim.

'*Go away, Tommy,*' Jim said feebly, '*go away.*'

The dog bounded off after Dave, who was the only one in sight now; Andy had dropped behind a log, where he lay flat on his face, having suddenly remembered a picture of the Russo–Turkish war with a circle of Turks lying flat on their faces (as if they were ashamed) round a newly-arrived shell.

There was a small hotel or shanty on the creek, on the main road, not far from the claim. Dave was desperate; the time flew much faster in his stimulated imagination than it did in reality, so he made for the shanty. There were several casual bushmen on the verandah and in the bar; Dave rushed into the bar, banging the door behind him. '*My dog!*' he gasped, in reply to the astonished publican, '*the blanky retriever – he's got a live cartridge in his mouth.*' The retriever, finding the front door shut against him, had bounded round and in by the back way, and now stood smiling in the doorway leading from the passage, the cartridge still in his mouth and the fuse spluttering. They burst out of that bar. Tommy bounded first after one and then after another, for, being a young dog, he tried to make friends with everybody.

The bushmen ran round corners, and some shut themselves in the stable. There was a new weatherboard and corrugated iron kitchen and wash-house on piles in the backyard, with some women washing clothes inside. Dave and the publican bundled in there and shut the door – the publican cursing Dave and calling him a crimson fool, in hurried tones, and wanting to know what the hell he came here for.

The retriever went in under the kitchen, amongst the piles, but, luckily for those inside, there was a vicious yellow mongrel cattle-dog sulking and nursing his nastiness under there – a sneaking, fighting, thieving canine, whom neighbours had tried for years to shoot or poison. Tommy saw his danger – he'd had experience from this dog – and started out across the yard, still sticking to the cartridge.

Halfway across the yard the yellow dog caught him and nipped him. Tommy dropped the cartridge, gave one terrified yell, and took to the Bush. The yellow dog followed him to the fence and then ran back to see what he had dropped. Nearly a dozen other dogs came from round all the corners and under the buildings – spidery, thievish, cold-blooded kangaroo dogs, mongrel sheep- and cattledogs, vicious black and yellow dogs – that slip after you in the dark, nip your heels, and vanish without explaining – and yapping, yelping small fry. They kept at a respectable distance round the nasty yellow dog, for it was dangerous to go near him when he thought he had found something which might be good for a dog or cat. He sniffed at the cartridge twice and was just taking a third cautious sniff when – It was very good blasting powder – a new brand that Dave had recently got up from Sydney; and the cartridge had been excellently well made. Andy was very patient and painstaking in all he did, and nearly as handy as the average sailor with needles, twine, canvas and rope.

Bushmen say that the kitchen jumped off its piles and on again. When the smoke and dust cleared away, the remains of the nasty yellow dog were lying against the paling fence of the yard looking as if he had been kicked into a fire by a horse and afterwards rolled in the dust under a barrow, and finally thrown against the fence from a distance. Several saddle horses, which had been 'hanging up' round the verandah, were galloping wildly down the road in clouds of dust, with broken bridle reins flying; and from a circle round the outskirts, every point of the compass in the scrub, came the yelping of dogs. Two of them went home to the place where they were born, thirty miles away, and reached it the same night and stayed there; it was not till towards evening that the rest came cautiously back to make inquiries. One was trying to walk on two legs, and most of 'em looked more or less singed; and a little, singed, stumpy-tailed dog, who had been in the habit of hopping the back half of him along on one leg, had reason to be glad he'd saved up the other leg all those years, for he needed it now. There was one old one-eyed cattle-dog round that shanty for years afterwards, who couldn't stand the smell of a gun being cleaned. He it was who had taken an interest, only second to that of the yellow dog, in the cartridge. Bushmen said that it was amusing to slip up on his blind side and stick a dirty ramrod under his nose; he wouldn't wait to bring his solitary eye to bear – he'd take to the bush and stay out all night.

For half an hour or so after the explosion there were several bushmen round behind the stable who crouched, doubled up, against the wall, or rolled gently on the dust, trying to laugh without shrieking. There were two white women in hysterics in the house, and a half-caste rushing aimlessly round with a dipper of cold water. The publican was holding his wife tight and begging her between squawks, to '*hold up for my sake, Mary, or I'll lam the life out of ye.*'

Dave decided to apologise later on, '*when things had settled down a bit*', and went back to camp. And the dog that had done it all, Tommy, the great idiotic mongrel retriever, came slobbering round Dave and lashing his legs with his tail, and trotted home after him, smiling his broadest, longest, and reddest smile of amiability, and apparently satisfied for one afternoon with the fun he'd had.

Andy chained up the dog securely, and cooked more chops, while Dave went to help Jim out of the hole.

And most of this is why, for years afterwards, lanky, easygoing bushmen, riding lazily past Dave's camp, would cry, in a lazy drawl and with just a hint of the nasal twang:

'Ello, Da-a-ave! How's the fishin' getting on, Da-a-ave?'

• WHEN THE WOLF WAS • AT THE DOOR

STEELE RUDD

There had been a long stretch of dry weather, and we were cleaning out the waterhole. Dad was down the hole shovelling up the dirt; Joe squatted on the brink catching flies and letting them go again without their wings, a favourite amusement of his; while Dan and Dave cut a drain to turn the water that ran off the ridge into the hole – when it rained. Dad was feeling dry, and told Joe to fetch him a drink.

Joe said, *'See first if this cove can fly with only one wing.'* Then he went, but returned and said, *'There's no water in the bucket – Mother used the last drop to boil the punkins,'* and renewed the flycatching. Dad tried to spit, and was going to say something when Mother, half-way between the house and the waterhole, cried out the grasspaddock was all on fire. *'So it is, Dad,'* said Joe, slowly but surely dragging the head off a fly with a finger and thumb.

Dad scrambled out of the hole and looked. *'God God!'* was all he said. How he ran! All of us rushed after him except Joe – he couldn't run very well, because the day before he had ridden fifteen miles on a poor horse, bareback. When near the fire Dad stopped running to break a green bush. He hit upon a tough one. Dad was in a hurry. The bush wasn't. Dad swore and tugged with all his might. Then the bush broke and Dad fell heavily on his back and swore again.

To save the cockatoo-fence that was round the cultivation was what was troubling Dad.

Right and left we fought the fire with boughs. Hot! It was hellish hot! Whenever there was a lull in the wind we worked. Like a windmill! Dad's bough moved – and how he rushed for another when that was used up! Once we had the fire almost under control, but the wind rose again, and away went the flames higher and faster than ever.

'It's no use,' said Dad at last, placing his hand on his head and throwing down his bough. We did the same, then stood and watched the fence go. After supper we went out again and saw it still burning. Joe asked Dad if he didn't think it was a splendid sight. Dad didn't answer him; he didn't seem conversational that night.

We decided to put the fence up again. Dan had sharpened the axe with a broken file, and he and Dad were about to start when Mother asked them what was to be done about flour. She said she had shaken the bag to get enough to make scones for that morning's breakfast, and unless some was got somewhere there would be no bread for dinner.

Dad reflected, while Dan felt the edge on the axe with his thumb.

Dad said, *'Won't Mrs Dwyer let you have a dishful until we get some?'*

'No,' Mother answered, *'I can't ask her until we send back what we owe them.'*

Dad reflected again. *'The Andersons, then?'* he said.

Mother shook her head and asked what good there was in sending to them when they, only that morning, had sent to her for some.

'Well, we must do the best we can at present,' Dad answered, *'and I'll go to the store this evening and see what is to be done.'*

Putting the fence up again, in the hurry that Dad was in, was the very devil! He felled the saplings – and such saplings – trees many of them were – while we, all of a muck of sweat, dragged them into line. Dad worked like a horse himself and expected us to do the same. *'Never mind staring about you,'* he'd say, if he caught us looking at the sun to see if it were coming dinner-time. *'There's no time to lose if we want to get the fence up and crop in.'*

Dan worked nearly as hard as Dad until he dropped the butt-end of a heavy sapling on his foot, which made him hop about on one leg and say that he was sick and tired of the dashed fence. Then he argued with Dad, and declared that it would be far better to put a wire fence up at once, and be done with it, instead of wasting time over a thing that would only be burnt down again. *'How long,'* he said, *'will it take to get the posts? Not a week,'* and he hit the ground disgustedly with a piece of stick he had in his hand.

'Confound it!' Dad said. *'Haven't you got any sense, boy? What earthly use would a wire fence be without any wire in it?'*

Then we knocked off and went to dinner.

No one appeared in any humour to talk at the table. Mother sat silently at the end and poured out the tea while Dad, at the head, served the pumpkin and divided what cold meat there was. Mother wouldn't have any meat – one of us would have to go without if she had taken any.

I don't know if it was on account of Dan's arguing with him, or if it was because there was no bread for dinner, that Dad was in a bad temper. Anyway, he swore at Joe for coming to the table with dirty hands. Joe cried and said that he couldn't wash them when Dave, as soon as he had washed his, had thrown the water out. Then Dad scowled at Dave, and Joe passed his plate along for more pumpkin.

Dinner was almost over when Dan, still looking hungry, grinned and asked Dave if he wasn't going to have some bread. Whereupon Dad jumped up in a tearing passion, *'Damn your insolence!'* he said to Dan. *'Make a jest of it, would you?'*

'Who's jestin'?' Dan answered and grinned again.

'Go!' said Dad furiously, pointing to the door. *'Leave my roof, you thankless dog!'*

Dan went that night.

It was only when Dad promised faithfully to reduce his account within two months that the storekeeper let us have another bag of flour on credit. And what a change that bag of flour wrought! How cheerful the place became all at once! And how enthusiastically Dad spoke of the farm and the prospects of the coming season!

Four months had gone by. The fence had been up some time and ten acres of wheat had been put in; but there had been no rain, and not a grain had come up, or was likely to.

Nothing had been heard of Dan since his departure. Dad spoke about him to Mother. *'The scamp,'* he said, *'to leave me just when I wanted help. After all the years I've slaved to feed him and clothe him, see what thanks I get! But, mark my word, he'll be glad to come back yet.'* But Mother would never say anything against Dan.

The weather continued dry. The wheat didn't come up, and Dad became despondent again.

The storekeeper called every week and reminded Dad of his promise. *'I would give it to you willingly,'* Dad would say, *'if I had it, Mr Rice, but what can I do? You can't knock blood out of a stone.'*

We ran short of tea and Dad thought to buy more with the money Anderson owed him for some fencing he had done. But when he asked for it, Anderson was very sorry he hadn't got it just then, but promised to let him have it as soon as he could sell his chaff. When Mother heard Anderson couldn't pay she did cry, and said there wasn't a bit of sugar in the house, or enough cotton to mend the children's bits of clothes.

We couldn't very well go without tea, so Dad showed Mother how to make a new kind. He roasted a slice of bread on the fire till it was like a black coal, then poured the boiling water over it and let it draw well. Dad said it had a capital flavour – he liked it.

Dave's only pair of pants were pretty well worn off him; Joe hadn't a decent coat for Sunday; Dad himself wore a pair of boots with the soles tied on with wire; and Mother fell sick. Dad did all he could – waited on her, and talked hopefully of the fortune which would come to us some day – but once, when talking to Dave, he broke down, and said he didn't, in the name of the Almighty God, know what he would do. Dave couldn't say anything – he moped about, too, and home somehow didn't seem like home at all.

When Mother was sick and Dad's time was mostly taken up nursing her, when there was hardly anything in the house, when in fact the wolf was at the very door, Dan came home with a pocket full of money and a swag full of greasy clothes. How Dad shook him by the hand and welcomed him back! And how Dan talked of tallies, bellywool, and ringers, and implored Dad, over and over again, to go shearing or rolling up, or branding – anything rather than work and starve on the selection.

But Dad stayed on the farm.

◆ GOING BLIND ◆

HENRY LAWSON

I met him in the Full-and-Plenty dining rooms, it was a cheap place in the city, with good beds upstairs let at one shilling per night – 'Board and residence for respectable single men, fifteen shillings per week'. I was a respectable single man then. I boarded and resided there. I boarded at a greasy little table in the greasy little corner under the fluffy little staircase in the hot and greasy little dining-room or restaurant downstairs. They called it dining-rooms, but it was only one room, and there wasn't half enough room in it to work your elbows when the seven little tables and forty-nine chairs were occupied. There was not room for an ordinary-sized steward to pass up and down between the tables; but our waiter was not an ordinary-sized man – he was a living skeleton in miniature. We handed the soup, and the *'roast beef one'* and *'roast lamb one'*, *'corn beef and cabbage one'*, *'veal and pickled pork one'* – or two, or three, as the case may be – and the tea and coffee, and the various kinds of pudding – we handed over each other, and dodged the drops as well as we could. The very hot and very greasy little kitchen was adjacent, and it contained the bathroom and other conveniences, behind screens of whitewashed boards.

I resided upstairs in a room where there were five beds and one wash-stand; one candle-stick, with a very short bit of soft yellow candle in it; the back of a hair-brush, with about a dozen bristles in it; and half a comb – the big tooth end – with nine and a half teeth at irregular distances apart.

He was a typical bushman, not one of those tall, straight, wiry, brown men of the West, but from the old selection districts, where many drovers came from, and of the old bush school; one of those slight, active little fellows whom we used to see in cabbage-tree hats, Crimean shirts, strapped trousers, and elastic-side boots – '*larstins*,' they called them. They could dance well, sing indifferently, and mostly through their noses, the old bush songs; play the concertina horribly; and ride like – like – well, they could ride.

He seemed as if he had forgotten to grow old and die out with this old colonial school to which he belonged. They had careless and forgetful ways about them. His name was Jack Gunther, he said, and he'd come to Sydney to try to get something done to his eyes. He had a portmanteau, a carpet bag, some things in a three-bushel bag, and a tin box. I sat beside him on his bed, and struck up an acquaintance, and he told me all about it. First he asked me would I mind shifting round to the other side, as he was rather deaf in that ear. He'd been kicked on the side of the head by a horse, he said, and had been a little dull o' hearing on that side ever since.

He was as good as blind. '*I can see the people near me,*' he said, '*but I can't make out their faces. I can just make out the pavement and the houses close at hand, and all the rest is a sort of white blur.*' He looked up: '*That ceiling is kind of white, ain't it? And this,*' tapping the wall and putting his nose close to it, '*is a sort of green, ain't it.*' The ceiling might have been whiter. The prevalent tints of the wallpaper had originally been blue and red, but it was mostly green enough now – a damp, rotten green; but I was ready to swear that the ceiling was snow and that the walls were as green as grass if it would have made him feel more comfortable. His sight began to get bad about six years before, he said; he didn't take much notice of it at first, and then he saw a quack, who made his eyes worse. He had already the manner of the blind – the touch in every finger, and even the gentleness in his speech. He had a boy down with him – a '*sorter cousin of his*' – and the boy saw him round. '*I'll have to be sending that youngster back,'* he said. *'I think I'll send him home next week. He'll be picking up and learning too much down here.'*

I happened to know the district he came from, and we would sit by the hour and talk about the country, and chaps by the name of this and chaps by the name of that – drovers mostly, whom we had met or had heard of. He asked me if I'd ever heard of a chap by the name of Joe Scott – a big, sandy-complexioned chap, who might be droving; he was his brother, or, at least, his half-brother, but he hadn't heard of him for years; he'd last heard of him at Blackall, in Queensland; he might have gone overland to Western Australia with Tyson's cattle to the new country.

We talked about grubbing and fencing and digging and droving and shearing – all about the bush – and it all came back to me as we talked. 'I can see it all now,' he said once, in an abstracted tone, seeming to fix his helpless eyes on the wall opposite. But he didn't see the dirty blind wall, nor the dingy window, nor the skimpy little bed, nor the greasy wash-stand: he saw the dark blue ridges in the sunlight, the grassy sidings and flats, the creek with clumps of she-oak here and there, the course of the willow-fringed river below, the distant peaks and ranges fading away into a lighter azure; the granite ridge in the middle distance, and the rocky rises, the stringy-bark and the apple-tree flats, the shrubs, and the sunlit plains – and all. I could see it too – plainer than I ever did.

He had done a bit of fencing in his time, and we got talking about timber. He didn't believe in having fencing-posts with big butts; he reckoned it was a mistake. *'You see,'* he said, *'the top of the butt catches the rain water and make the post rot quicker. I'd back posts without any butt at all to last as long or longer than posts with 'em – that's if the post is well put up and well rammed.'* He had supplied fencing stuff, and fenced by contract, and – well, you can get more posts without butts out of a tree than posts with them. He also objected to charring the butts. He said it only made work, and wasted time – the butts lasted longer without being charred.

I asked him if he'd ever got stringy-bark palings or shingles out of mountain ash, and he smiled a smile that did my heart good to see, and said he had. He had also got them out of various other kinds of trees.

We talked about soil and grass, and gold-digging, and many other things which came back to one like a revelation as we yarned.

He had been to the hospital several times. *'The doctors don't say they can cure me,'* he said; *'they say they might be able to improve my sight and hearing, but it would take a long time – anyway, the treatment would improve my general health. They know what's the matter with my eyes,'* and he explained it as well as he could. *'I wish I'd seen a good doctor when my eyes first began to get weak; but young chaps are always careless over things. It's harder to get cured of anything when you're done growing.'*

He was always hopeful and cheerful. *'If the worst comes to the worst,'* he said, *'there's things I can do where I come from. I might do a bit o' wool-sorting, for instance. I'm a pretty fair expert. Or else when they're weeding out I could help. I'd just have to sit down and they'd bring the sheep to me, and I'd feel the wool and tell them what it was – being blind improves the feeling, you know.'*

He had a packet of portraits, but he couldn't make them out very well now. They were sort of blurred to him, but I described them, and he told me who they were. *'That's a girl o' mine,'* he said, with reference to one – a jolly, good-looking bush girl. *'I got a letter from her yesterday. I managed to scribble something, but I'll get you, if you don't mind, to write something more I want to put in on another piece of paper, and address an envelope for me.'*

Darkness fell quickly upon him now – or, rather, the *'sort of white blur'* increased and closed in. But his hearing was better, he said, and he was glad of that and still cheerful. I thought it natural that his hearing should improve as he went blind.

One day he said that he did not think he would bother going to the hospital any more. He reckoned he'd get back to where he was known. He'd stayed down too long already, and the *'stuff'* wouldn't stand it. He was expecting a letter that didn't come. I was away for a couple of days, and when I came back he had been shifted out of the room, and had a bed in an angle of the landing on top of the staircase, with people brushing against him and stumbling over his things all day on their way up and down. I felt indignant, thinking that – the house being full – the boss had taken advantage of the bushman's helplessness and good nature to put him there. But he said that he was quite comfortable. *'I can get a whiff of air here,'* he said.

Going in next day I thought for a moment that I had dropped suddenly back into the past and into a bush dance, for there was a concertina going upstairs. He was sitting on the bed, with his legs crossed, and a new cheap concertina on his knee, and his eyes turned to the patch of ceiling as if it were a piece of music and he could read it. *'I'm trying to knock a few tunes into my head,'* he said, with a brave smile, *'in case the worst comes to the worst.'* He tried to be cheerful, but seemed worried and anxious. The letter hadn't come. I thought of the many blind musicians in Sydney, and I thought of the bushman's chance, standing at a corner swanking a cheap concertina, and I felt very sorry for him.

I went out with a vague idea of seeing someone about the matter, and getting something done for the bushman – of bringing a little influence to his assistance; but I suddenly remembered that my clothes were worn out, my hat in a shocking state, my boots burst, and that I owed for a week's board and lodging, and was likely to be thrown out at any moment myself; and so I was not in a position to go where there was influence.

When I went back to the restaurant there was a long, gaunt, sandy-complexioned bushman sitting by Jack's side. Jack introduced him as his brother, who had returned unexpectedly to his native district, and had followed him to Sydney. The brother was rather short with me at first, and seemed to regard the restaurant people – all of us, in fact – in the light of spielers, who wouldn't hesitate to take advantage of Jack's blindness if he left him a moment; and he looked ready to knock down the first man who stumbled across Jack, or over his luggage – but that soon wore off. Jack was going to stay with Joe at the Coffee Palace for a few weeks, and then go up country, he told me. He was excited and happy. His brother's manner towards him was as if Jack had just lost his wife, or boy, or someone very dear to him. He would not allow him to do anything for himself, nor try to – not even lace up his boots. He seemed to think that he was thoroughly helpless, and when I saw him pack up Jack's things, and help him at the table, and fix his tie and collar with his great muscular hands, which trembled all the time with grief and gentleness, and make Jack sit down on the bed whilst he got a cab and carried the traps down to it, and take him downstairs as if he were made of thin glass, and settle the landlord – then I knew Jack was all right.

We had a drink together – Joe, Jack, the cabman and I. Joe was very careful to hand Jack the glass, and Jack made a joke about it for Joe's benefit. He swore he could see a glass yet, and Joe laughed, but looked extra troubled the next moment.

I felt their grips on my hand for five minutes after we parted.

◆ A VISIT TO ◆ SCRUBBY CREEK

EDWARD DYSON

The men at the mine were anxious to have me visit our magnificent property. The battery and water-wheel were erected, there were fifty tons of stone in the hopper, and we only needed water and the blessing of Providence to start crushing out big weekly dividends. I know now that there has never been a time within the memory of man when Scrubby Gully did not want water, and that Scrubby Gully is the one place on earth to which a discriminating man would betake himself if he wished to avoid all the blessings of Providence forever. But that is beside the matter.

I was carefully instructed by letter to take the train to Kanan, coach it to the Rabbit Trap, take horse from Whalan's to the Cross Roads, ask someone at Old Poley's on the hill to direct me to Sheep's Eye; from there strike west on foot, keeping Bugle Point on my right, and 'Chin Whiskers' would meet me at The Crossing. There was no accommodation at the mine for city visitors; but I was given to understand Mr Larry Jeans would be happy to accommodate me at his homestead over the spur.

Casual references to Mr Jeans in the correspondence gave me the impression that Jeans was an affluent gentleman of luxurious tastes and a hospitable disposition, and that a harmless eccentricity led him to follow agricultural and pastoral pursuits in the vicinity of Scrubby Gully instead of wasting his time in voluptuous ease in the city.

'Chin Whiskers' met me at The Crossing. 'Chin Whiskers' was

a meditative giant who exhausted his mental and physical energies chewing tobacco, and who bore about his person interesting and obvious evidence of the length and severity of the local drought – he was in fact, the drought incarnate. The Crossing was a mere indication of a track across a yellow rock-strewn indentation between two hills, which indentation, 'Chin Whiskers' informed me, was 'The Creek'. That did not surprise me, because I knew that every second country township and district in Australia has a somewhat similar indentation which it always calls 'The Creek'. Sometimes 'The Creek' has moist places in it, sometimes it is quite damp for almost a dozen miles, but more often it is as hard and dry as a brick-kiln. When the indentation is really wet along its whole length it is invariably called 'The River'.

I found the mine: it was a simple horizontal hole bored in a hill. The battery was there, and the water-wheel. The water-wheel stood disconsolate beside the dust-strewn creek, and looked as much at home as a water-wheel might be expected to look in the centre of the sandy wastes of the Sahara. The working shareholders were unaffectedly glad to see me. They were sapless and drought-stricken, but they assured me, with great enthusiasm, that they lived in momentary expectation of a tremendous downfall. Leen had been mending the roof of his hut, he said, in readiness for the heavy rains which were due before morning. He examined the sky critically, and expressed a belief that I would be detained on Scrubby Gully a couple of weeks or so in consequence of the floods.

This spirit of unreasonable hopefulness and trust seemed to be shared by Cody, and Ellis and MacMahon. I alone was dubious. The journey up had worn me out; the dry desolation all around and the flagrant unprofitableness of our spec sickened me; but Jeans still remained – the prodigal Jeans, with his spacious homestead and profuse hospitality. I was heartily grateful for Jeans. We met in due course.

As I talked with Leen, a man came wearily down the hill, towing a meagre horse, which in turn was towing a log. This man delivered his log, unslung his animal, and approached us, heroically lugging behind him the miserable apology for a horse – a morbid brute manifestly without a hope or ambition left in life, and conveying mysteriously to the observer a knowledge of its fixed and unshakable determination to lie down and die the moment its owner's attention was otherwise directed. But the proprietor seemed fully alive to the situation, and never allowed his thoughts to stray entirely from the horse, but was continually jerking its head up, and addressing towards it reproaches, expostulations, and curses – curses that had lost all their vigour and dignity. This man was Jeans, and if I had not seen his horse I would have said that Jeans was the most hopelessly heart-broken and utterly used-up animal breathing on the face of the earth. He was about forty, grey, hollow-cheeked, hollow-chested, bent, and apathetic with the dreadful apathy that comes of wasted effort, vain toil, and blasted hopes. Jeans had a face that had forgotten how to smile and never scowled – a face that took no exercise, but remained set in the one wooden expression of joyless, passionless indifference to whatever fate could offer henceforth and forever. My last hope exploded at the sight of him.

Mr Larry Jeans said I was welcome to camp in the spare room '*up to*' his place, and added dully that '*proberly*' his missus could scrape up grub enough for me '*fer a day'r two*'. '*Proberly*' did not sound very encouraging, but I had no option, and being dead-beat, accepted the hospitality offered, and followed Mr Jeans. Larry laboriously hauled his melancholy horse over a couple of low stony rises, and then we tackled the scrag end of the range, across which led a vague track that wound in and out amongst a forest of great rocks, and presented all the difficulties and dangers of mountaineering without its compensations.

Jeans struggled on with dull patience, and in silence, saving when it was necessary to divert the old horse from his morbid thoughts, and when he briefly answered my questions. I gathered from him that the men at the mine had been expecting rain for four months.

'And what do you think of the chances?' I asked.

'Oh, me, I never expect nothin'. Sometimes things happen. I don't expect 'em, though.'

'Things happen – what, for instance?'

'Well, dry spells.'

I elicited that pleuro happened, and rabbits, and fires, and 'this here new-fangled fever'. But whatever happened Jeans never fluctuated; he had struck an average of misery, and was bogged in the moral slough. It seemed as if his sensibilities above a certain capacity had been worn out by over-work, and refused to feel more than a fixed degree of trouble, so that whatever might come on top of his present woes, be it fever, or fire, or death, the man remained in his normal condition of grim apathy and spiritless obedience to fate.

The 'homestead' stood upon the flat timbered country beyond the rise. It was just what Jeans's homestead might have been expected to be – a low structure of bark and slabs, with a chimney at one end, and a door in the middle between two canvas 'windows'. It stood in a small clearing; just beyond the house stood the skeleton of a shed, upon which, it being sundown, roosted a few gaunt fowls; a lank cow with one horn was deeply meditating by the front door. There were signs of bold raids upon the stubborn bush, pathetic ventures; and great butts lay about in evidence of much weary, unprofitable work. A dog-leg fence, starting at no particular point, straddled along in front of the house, and finished nowhere, a hundred yards off. With much dry grass matted amongst the logs – that was the pathos of it. There had been a brave attempt at a garden, too; but the few fruit trees that stood had been stripped of the bark, and then hens had made dust-baths in all the beds. In this dust an army of children were wallowing – half-clad, bare-footed, dirt-encrusted children, but all hale and boisterous.

At the door we were met by Mrs Larry Jeans, and after introducing me as 'him from the city', the master laboured away, dragging his shuffling horse, and leaving me in the centre of a wondering circle of youngsters of all sorts and sizes, from two dusty mites not yet properly balanced on their crooked little legs to a shock-headed lubberly boy of thirteen, curiously embossed with large tan freckles, and a tall, gawky girl of the same age in preposterously short skirts, whom my presence afflicted with a most painful bashfulness. A peculiarity about Jeans's children that struck me was the fact that they seemed to run in sets; there was a pair even for the sticky baby deftly hooked under its mother's left arm, judging by the petulant wailing to be heard within.

The Jeans's homestead consisted of two compartments. I looked about in vain for the *'spare room'*, and concluded it must be either the capacious fire-place or the skeleton shed on which the hens were roosting. The principal article of kitchen furniture was a long plank table built into the floor; between it and the wall was a bush-made form, also a fixture. A few crazy three-legged stools, a safe manufactured from a zinc-lined case, and an odd assortment of crockery and tin cups, saucers and plates piled on slab shelves in one corner, completed the list of *'fixings'*.

Mrs Larry Jeans was a short, bony, homely woman, very like her husband – strangely, pathetically, like in face and demeanour; similarly bowed with labour, and with the same air of hopelessness and of accepting the toils and privations of their miserable existence as an inevitable lot. She was always working, and always had worked; her hands were hard and contorted in evidence of it, and her cheek was as brown and dry as husks from labouring in the sun.

We had tea and bread and boiled onions and corned beef for tea that evening – a minimum of beef and a maximum of onions. The last onion crop had been a comparative success somewhere within half a day's journey to Scrubby Gully. Tea served to introduce more children; they dangled over the arms of the unhappy mother, hung to her skirts, sprawled about her feet, squabbled in the corners, and overran the house. Jeans helped to feed the brood in his slow, patient way, and after tea he helped to pack away the younger in little bundles – here, there, and everywhere – where they slept peacefully, but in great apparent peril, whilst the bigger kids charged around the room and roared, and fought, and raised a very real pandemonium of their own. Every now and again Mrs Jeans would lift her tired head from her sewing or her insatiable twins, and say weakly, *'Now, you Jinny, behave.'* Or Larry would remark dispassionately, *'Hi, you, Billy!'* But otherwise the youngsters raged unchecked, their broken-spirited parents seeming to regard the noise and worry of them as the lightest trial in a world of struggling and trouble.

I asked Jeans how many children he thought he had. He didn't seem certain, but after due deliberation said there might be thirteen in all. He had probably lost count, for I am certain I tallied fifteen – seven sets and one odd one.

When the washing-up was done, and half of the family were bedded down, Larry dragged a tangle of old harness from the corner of the room, and sat for two hours painfully piecing it up with cord, and his wife sat opposite him, silent and blank of face, mending one set of rags with another – I perched upon a stool watching the pair, studying one face after the other, irritated by the length of the sheep-like immobility of both, thinking it would be a relief if Jeans would suddenly break out and do something desperate, something to show that he had not, in spite of appearances, got beyond the possibility of sanguinary revolt, but he worked on steadily, uncomplainingly, till the boy with the unique freckles came hurrying in with the intelligence that the old horse was *'havin' a fit'r somethin'.* Jeans did not swear. He said, *'Is he but?'* and put aside his harness, and went out, like a man for whom life has no surprises.

The selector was over an hour struggling with his hypochondriac horse, while I exchanged fragments of conversation with Mrs Jeans, and went upon various mental excursions after that spare room. It appeared that the Jeanses had neighbours. There was another family settled seven miles up the gully, but Mrs Jeans informed me that the Dicksons, being quiet and sort of down-hearted, were not very good company, consequently she and Jeans rarely visited them. I was indulging in a mental prospect of the jubilation at a reunion of the down-hearted Dicksons and the gay and frivolous Jeanses when Larry returned from his struggle with the horse. He resumed his work upon the harness without any complaint. His remark that *'Them skewball horses is alwis onreasonable'* was not spoken in a carping spirit; it was given as conveying valuable information to a stranger.

At eleven o'clock my host *'s'posed that p'raps maybe'* I was ready to turn in. I was, and we went forth together in quest of the spare room. The room in question proved to be a hastily-constructed lean-to on the far corner of the house, at the back. Inside, one wall was six feet high and the other was merely a tree-butt. My bunk was against the butt, and between the bunk and the roof were about eighteen inches of space. That bunk had not been run up for a fat man. After establishing me in the spare room Jeans turned to go.

'Best bar the door with a log, case o' the cow,' he said. *'If she comes bumpin' round in the night, don't mind. She walks in her sleep moonlit nights.'*

It only needed this to convince me that I was usurping the customary domicile of the meditative cow. The room had been carefully furbished up and deeply carpeted with scrub ferns. But the cow was not to be denied.

Weary as I was, I got little sleep that night. I had fallen off comfortably about half an hour after turning in, when I was awakened again by some commotion in the house. Half a dozen of the children were blubbering, and I could hear the heavy tread of Larry, and the equally heavy tread of his wife, moving about the house. Presently both passed by the lean-to, and away in the direction of the range. For another half-hour or so there was silence, and then the one-horned cow came along and tried my door. Failing to open it, she tried the walls and the roof, but could not break her way in, so she camped under the lee of the structure, and lowed dismally at intervals till daybreak.

When I arose a scantily attired small boy generously provided me with a pint pannikin three-parts full of water. The water was for my morning bath, and the small boy was careful to warn me not to throw it away when I was through with it. This youngster told me that 'Dad an' Mum, and Jimmy' had been out all night hunting Steve. Steve, I gathered, was the one enterprising child in the household, and was in the habit of going alone upon voyages of exploration along the range, where, being a very little fellow, he usually lost himself, and provided his parents with a night's entertainment searching for him in the barren gorges and about the boulder-strewn spurs of the range. How it happened that he was not missed till nearly midnight on this occasion I cannot say, unless the father and mother were really as ignorant of the extent and character of their family as they appeared to be.

Mrs Jeans was the first to return, and she brought Steve with her. The dear child had not been lost, after all. Incensed by some indignity that had been put upon him during the afternoon, he had 'run away from home', he said, and slept all night in a wombat's hole about two hundred yards from the house. There his mother found him, returning from her long, weary search. The incident did not appear to have affected her in any way; she looked as tired and heart-sick as on the previous evening, but not more so.

'*You know we lost one little one there*' – she extended her hand towards the low, rambling, repellent hills – '*an' found him dead a week after.*'

Larry returned half an hour later, and his apathy under the circumstances was simply appalling.

We had fried onions and bread and tea for breakfast, and immediately after the meal was over Larry, who I imagined would be going to bed for a few hours, appeared in front of the house leading his deplorable horse. He was bound for the mine, he said. I put in that day exploring the tunnel, examining the immovable mill, hunting for specimens in the quartz-tip, and listening to Leen's cheerful weather prophecies; and Jeans and his soured quadruped dragged logs to the mine from a patch of timber about a mile off, which patch the men alluded to largely as The Gum Forest.

Returning to the homestead at sundown we found the children fighting in the dust and the one-horned cow meditating at the door as on the previous evening. I fancied I detected in the eye of the cow a look of pathetic reproach as I passed her. Tea that evening consisted mainly of roast onions. Jeans felt called upon to apologise because the boys had been unable to trap a rabbit for my benefit.

'*Now'n agen, after a rainy spell, we're 'most afraid the rabbits is a-goin' to eat us, an' then when we'd like a rabbit-stoo there ain't a rabbit to be found within twenty mile,*' said the settler impassively. '*When there is rabbits, there ain't onions,*' he added as a further contribution to the curiosities of natural history.

The second night at Scrubby Gully was painfully like the first: Mrs Jeans stitched, Mr Jeans laboured over his tangle of harness, and the brood rolled and tumbled about the room, raising much dust and creating a deafening noise, to which Larry and Mary his wife gave little heed. When a section of the family had been parcelled up and put to sleep, I was tempted to ask Jeans why he continued to live in that unhallowed, out-of-the-way corner, and to waste his energies upon a parched and blasted holding instead of settling somewhere within reach of a market and beyond the blight of tangible and visible despair that hung over Scrubby Gully and its vicinity.

'Dunno,' said Jeans, without interest, 'pears to me t' be pretty much as bad in other places. Evans is the same, so's Calder.'

I did not know either Evans or Calder, but I pitied them from the bottom of my heart. Jeans admitted that he had given up hope of getting the timber off his land, though he 'suspected' he might be able to handle it somehow 'when the boys grew up'. He further admitted that he didn't know 'as the land was good for anythin' much' when it was cleared but his pessimism was proof against all arguments, and I went sadly to bunk, leaving the man and his wife working with slow, animal perseverance, apparently unconscious of the fact that they had not slept a wink for over thirty hours.

The cow raided my room shortly after midnight. She managed to break down the door this time, but as her intentions were peaceful, and as it was preferable rather to have her for a room-mate than to be kept awake by her pathetic complaints, I made no attempt to evict her, and we both passed an easy night.

I was up early next morning, but Mr and Mrs Jeans were before me. They were standing together down by the aimless dog-leg fence, and the hypochondriacal horse lay between them. I walked across, suspecting further 'unreasonableness' on the part of the horse. The animal was dead.

'Old man, how'll you manage to haul those logs in now?' As Mrs Jeans said this I fancied I saw flicker in her face for a moment a look of spiritual agony, a hint of revolt that might manifest itself in tears and bitter complainings, but it passed in the instant. Jeans merely shook his head, and answered something indicative of the complete destruction of faith in '*them skewbald horses*'.

We had bread and onions for breakfast.

When I last saw Jeans, as I was leaving Scrubby Gully that day, he was coming down the hill from the direction of the gum forest, struggling in the blinding heat, with a rope over his shoulder, towing a nine-foot sluice log.

We had a letter from Leen yesterday; he says the working shareholders are hurrying to get the sluice fixed over the wheel, and he *(Leen)* anticipates a heavy downfall of rain during the night.

• THAT THERE • DOG O' MINE

—————— HENRY LAWSON ——————

Macquarie the shearer had met with an accident. To tell the truth, he had been in a drunken row at a wayside shanty, from which he had escaped with three fractured ribs, a cracked head, and various minor abrasions. His dog, Tally, had been a sober but savage participator in the drunken row, and had escaped with a broken leg. Macquarie afterwards shouldered his swag and staggered and struggled along the track ten miles to the Union-Town hospital. Lord knows how he did it. He didn't exactly know himself. Tally limped behind all the way, on three legs.

The doctors examined the man's injuries and were surprised at his endurance. Even doctors are surprised sometimes – though they don't always show it. Of course they would take him in, but they objected to Tally. Dogs were not allowed on the premises.

'*You will have to turn that dog out,*' they said to the shearer, as he sat on the edge of a bed.

Macquarie said nothing.

'*We cannot allow dogs about the place, my man,*' said the doctor in a louder tone, thinking the man was deaf.

'*Tie him up in the yard then.*'

'*No. He must go out. Dogs are not permitted on the grounds.*'

Macquarie rose slowly to his feet, shut his agony behind his set teeth, painfully buttoned his shirt over his hairy chest, took up his waistcoat, and staggered to the corner where the swag lay.

'*What are you going to do?*' they asked.

'*You ain't going to let my dog stop?*'

'*No. It's against the rules. There are no dogs allowed on the premises.*'

He stooped and lifted his swag, but the pain was too great, and he leaned back against the wall.

'*Come, come now! man alive!*' exclaimed the doctor, impatiently, '*You must be mad. You know you are not in a fit state to go out. Let the wardsman help you undress.*'

'*No!*' said Macquarie. '*No. If you won't take my dog in you don't take me. He's got a broken leg and wants fixing up just – just as much as – as I do. If I'm good enough to come in, he's good enough – and – and better.*'

He paused awhile, breathing painfully, and then went on.

'*That – that there old dog of mine has follered me faithful and true, these twelve long hard and hungry years. He's about – the only thing that ever cared whether I lived or fell and rotted on the cursed track.*'

He rested again; then he continued; '*That – that there dog was pupped on the track,*' he said with a sad sort of smile. '*I carried him for months in a billy can and afterwards on my swag when he was knocked up … And the old slut – his mother – she'd foller along quite contented – sniff the billy now and again – just to see he was all right … She follered me for God knows how many years. She follered me till she was blind – and for a year after. She follered me till she could crawl along through the dust no longer, and – and then I killed her, because I couldn't leave her behind alive!*'

He rested again.

'*And this here old dog,*' he continued, touching Tally's upturned nose with his knotted finger, '*this here old dog has follered me for – for ten years; through floods and droughts, through fair times and – and hard – mostly hard; and kept me from going mad when I had no mate nor money on the lonely track; and watched over me for weeks when I was drunk – drugged and poisoned at the cursed shanties; and saved my life more'n once, and got kicks and curses* very often for thanks; and forgave me for it all; and – and fought for me. He was the only living thing that stood up for me against that crawling push of curs when they set onter me at the shanty back yonder – and he left his mark on some of 'em too; and – and so did I.'

He took another spell.

Then he drew his breath, shut his teeth hard, shouldered his swag, stepped into the doorway, and faced round again.

The dog limped out of the corner and looked up anxiously.

'That there dog,' said Macquarie to the hospital staff in general, 'is a better dog than I'm a man – or you too, it seems – and a better Christian. He's been a better mate to me than I ever was to any man – or any man to me. He's watched over me; kep' me from getting robbed many a time; fought for me; saved my life and took drunken kicks and curses for thanks – and forgave me. He's been a true, straight, honest, and faithful mate to me – and I ain't going to desert him now. I ain't going to kick him out in the road with a broken leg. I – Oh, my God! my back!'

He groaned and lurched forward, but they caught him, slipped off the swag, and laid him on a bed.

Half an hour later the shearer was comfortably fixed up. 'Where's my dog?' he asked, when he came to himself.

'Oh, the dog's all right,' said the nurse rather impatiently. 'Don't bother. The doctor's setting his leg out in the yard.'

◆ MITCHELL ◆
A CHARACTER SKETCH

———— HENRY LAWSON ————

It was a very mean station, and Mitchell thought he had better go himself and beard the overseer for tucker. His mates were for waiting till the overseer went out on the run, and then trying their luck with the cook; the self-assertive and diplomatic Mitchell decided to go.

'Good day,' said Mitchell.

'Good day,' said the manager.

'It's hot,' said Mitchell.

'I don't suppose,' said Mitchell, 'but I don't suppose you want any fencing done?'

'Naw.'

'Nor boundary riding?'

'Naw.'

'You ain't likely to want a man to knock around?'

'Naw.'

'I thought not. Things are pretty bad just now.'

'Na – yes – they are.'

'Ah, well; there's a lot to be said on the squatter's side as well as on the men's. I suppose I can get a bit of rations?'

'Ye-yes.' (Shortly) – 'Wot d'yer want?'

'Well, let's see; we want a bit of meat and flour – I think that's all. Got enough tea and sugar to carry us on.'

'All right. Cook! have you got any meat?'

'No!'

To Mitchell: *'Can you kill a sheep?'*

'Rather!'

To the cook: *'Give this man a cloth and knife and steel, and let him go up to the yard and kill a sheep.'* (To Mitchell): *'You can take a fore-quarter and get a bit of flour.'*

Half an hour later Mitchell came back with the carcass wrapped in the cloth …

'Here yer are: here's your sheep,' he said to the cook.

'That's all right; hang it in there. Did you take a fore-quarter?'

'No.'

'Well, why didn't you? The boss told you to.'

'I didn't want a forequarter. I don't like it. I took a hindquarter.'

So he had.

The cook scratched his head; he seemed to have nothing to say. He thought about trying to think, perhaps, but gave it best. It was too hot and he was out of practice.

'Here, fill these up, will you?' said Mitchell. *'That's the teabag, and that's the sugar bag, and that's the flour bag.'*

He had taken them from the front of his shirt.

'Don't be frightened to stretch 'em a little, old man. I've got two mates to feed.'

The cook took the flour bags mechanically and filled them well before he knew what he was doing. Mitchell talked all the time.

'Thank you,' said he – *'got a bit of baking-powder?'*

'Ye – yes, here you are.'

'Thank you. Find it dull here, don't you?'

'Well, yes, pretty dull. There's a bit of cooked beef and some bread and cake there, if you want it!'

'Thanks,' said Mitchell, sweeping the broken victuals into an old pillow-slip which he carried on his person for an emergency. *'I s'pose*

you find it dull round her.'

'Yes, pretty dull.'

'No one to talk to much?'

'No, not many.'

'Tongue gets rusty?'

'Ye – es sometimes.'

'Well, so long, and thank yer.'

'So long,' said the cook (he nearly added 'thank yer').

'Well, good day; I'll see you again.'

'Good day.'

Mitchell shouldered the spoil and left.

The cook scratched his head; he had a chat with the overseer afterwards, and they agreed that the traveller was a bit gone.

But Mitchell wasn't gone – not much; he was a Sydney jackaroo who had been round a bit – that was all.

◆ STARTING ◆ THE SELECTION

STEELE RUDD

It's twenty years now since we settled on the Creek. Twenty years! I remember well the day we came from Stanthorpe, on Jerome's dray – eight of us, and all the things – beds, tubs, a bucket, the two cedar chairs with pine bottoms and backs that Dad put in them, some pint-pots and old Crib. It was a scorching hot day, too – talk about thirst! At every creek we came to we drank till it stopped running.

Dad didn't travel up with us; he had gone some months before, to put up the house and dig the waterhole. It was a slabbed house, with shingled roof, and space enough for two rooms, but the partition wasn't up. The floor was earth, but Dad had a mixture of sand and fresh cow-dung with which he used to keep it level. About once every month he would put it on, and everyone had to keep outside that day till it was dry. There were no locks on the doors. Pegs were put in them to keep them fast at night, and the slabs were not very close together, for we could easily see anybody coming on horseback by looking through them. Joe and I used to play at counting the stars through the cracks in the roof.

The day after we arrived Dad took Mother and us out to see the paddock and the flat on the other side of the gully that he was going to clear for cultivation. There was no fence round the paddock, but he pointed out on a tree the surveyor's marks showing the boundary of our ground. It must have been fine land, the way Dad talked about it. There was very valuable timber on it, too, he said; and he showed us a place among some rocks on a ridge where he was sure gold would be found, but we weren't to say anything about it. Joe and I went back that evening and turned over every stone on the ridge, but we didn't find any gold.

No mistake, it was a real wilderness – nothing but trees, goannas, dead timber, and bears; and the nearest house, Dwyer's, was three miles away. I often wonder how the women stood it the first few years, and I can remember how Mother, when she was alone, used to sit on a log where the lane is now and cry for hours. Lonely! It was lonely.

Dad soon talked about clearing a couple of acres and putting in corn – all of us did, in fact – till the work commenced. It was a delightful topic before we started, but in two weeks the clusters of fires that illuminated the whooping bush in the night, and the crash upon crash of the big trees as they fell, had lost all their poetry.

We toiled and toiled clearing those four acres, where the haystacks are now standing, till every tree and sapling that had grown there was down. We thought then the worst was over – but how little we knew of clearing land! Dad was never tired of calculating and telling us how much the crop would fetch if the ground could only be got ready in time to put it in; so we laboured the harder.

With our combined male and female forces and the aid of a sapling lever we rolled the thundering big logs together in the face of hell's own fires; and when there were no logs to roll it was tramp, tramp the day through, gathering armfuls of sticks, while the clothes clung to our backs with a muddy perspiration. Sometimes Dan and Dave would sit in the shade beside the billy of water and gaze at the small patch that had taken so long to do, then they would turn hopelessly to what was before them and ask Dad (who would never take a spell) what was the use of ever getting such a place cleared. And when Dave wanted to know why Dad didn't take up a place on the plain, where there were no trees to grub and plenty of water, Dad would cough as if something was sticking in his throat, and then curse terribly the squatters and political jobbery. He would soon cool down, though, and get hopeful again.

'Look at the Dwyers,' he'd say. 'From ten acres of wheat they got seventy pounds last year, besides feed for the fowls. They've got corn in now, and there's only the two of them.'

It wasn't only burning off! Whenever there was a drought the waterhole was sure to run dry. Then we had to take turns to carry water from the springs – about two miles.

We had no draught horse, and even if we had had one there was neither water-cask, trolly, nor dray. So we humped it – and talk about a dray! By the time you returned, if you hadn't drained the bucket, in spite of the big drink you'd take before leaving the springs, more than half would certainly be spilt through the vessel bumping against your leg every time you stumbled in long grass. Somehow, none of us liked carrying water. We would sooner keep the fires going all day without dinner than do a trip to the springs.

One hot, thirsty day it was Joe's turn with the bucket, and he managed to get back without spilling very much. We were all pleased because there was enough left after the tea had been made to give us all a drink. Dinner was nearly over. Dan had finished and was taking it easy on the sofa when Joe said, 'I say, Dad, what's a nater-dog like?'

Dad told him. 'Yellow, sharp ears and bushy tail.'

'Those muster been some then that I seen – I don't know 'bout the bushy tail – all the hair had comed off.'

'Where'd y'see them, Joe?' we asked.

'Down the springs floating about – dead.'

Then everyone seemed to think hard and look at the tea. I didn't want any more. Dan jumped off the sofa and went outside; and Dad looked after Mother.

At last the four acres – except for the biggest iron-bark trees and about fifty stumps – were pretty well cleared. Then came a problem that couldn't be worked out on a draught-board. I have already said that we hadn't any draught-horses. Indeed, the only thing on the selection like a horse was an old *'tuppy'* mare that Dad used to straddle. The date of her foaling went farther back than Dad's, I believe, and she was shaped something like an alderman. We found her one day in about eighteen inches of mud, with both eyes picked out by the crows, and her hide bearing evidence that a feathery tribe made a roost of her carcass. Plainly, there was no chance of breaking up the ground with her help. And we had no plough. How, then, was the corn to be put in? That was the question.

Dan and Dave sat outside in the corner of the chimney, both scratching the ground with a chip and not saying anything. Dad and Mother sat inside talking it over. Sometimes Dad would get up and walk round the room shaking his head, then he would kick old Crib for lying under the table. At last Mother struck something which brightened him up, and he called Dave.

'*Catch Topsy and –*' he paused because he remembered the old mare was dead.

'*Run over and ask Mr Dwyer to lend me three hoes.*'

Dave went. Dwyer lent the hoes, and the problem was solved. That was how we started.

• ICONS •

HILL'S HOIST

New inventions are generally created out of need, and that is how the Hill's Hoist came into being. The year was 1945, and motor mechanic Lance Hill, from Adelaide, had been asked by his wife Sherry to make a washing line. Two orange trees that she had planted in their backyard had grown so big that she had begun to run out of clothes line space.

Rotary clothes lines were used widely in those days, but what was needed was a means of raising the washing after it had been hung out so that it would catch the breeze and dry faster. To do this Hill modified a car differential, and designed it so it could be operated by using a simple crank handle.

The first Hill's Hoist was rather crude, made from just a few lengths of steel tubing and a roll of galvanised wire. Crude though it was, it did the job it was designed to do.

After placing quite a modest advertisement in the Saturday paper Hill was inundated with orders. At that time a Hill's Hoist cost 10 guineas plus slightly more for installation. In 1946 Hill formed a partnership with his brother-in-law and began small-scale production, moving to mass hoist production in 1948.

Hill's invention proved very successful, making the chore of hanging out clothes a less onerous one for the millions of Australians who now have a Hill's Hoist in the backyard.

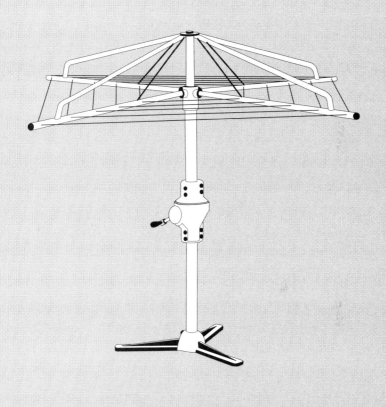

• ICONS •

THE UTE

Farmers years ago were in a bind when it came to buying a car. Although they needed something they could use to drive around the farm, they also needed a more comfortable car to take the whole family out for the day.

In 1932, a farmer's wife wrote to Ford in Geelong, Victoria, asking why a car couldn't be made to serve both purposes.

The task was handed to Lewis Bandt, the 22-year-old car designer for Ford Australia. In just two weeks Bandt had prepared life-size sketches of a car that would suit both farm and recreational uses, showing a car that was adapted from a new range of cars Ford had just released. The cars were different in that they had special strengthening at the rear so they wouldn't break when the load area filled to capacity.

Bandt was summoned to Detroit for a special viewing of the prototype by Henry Ford, who later described the ute as 'a kangaroo chaser'. Ten thousand pounds went in to produce an initial run of 500 utes, and a steady stream has poured out of the factory ever since. Now it's not just farmers who drive the ute, but also ordinary people who use the ute as their get-about car.

Bandt eventually retired from Ford Australia after 48 years of service, and with his new-found free time he built a replica of the very first ute. Sadly, in 1987 while driving the replica, he collided with a truck and died.

SLANG

• SLANG •

CONTENTS

SLANG-A-SAURUS
▼ ▼ ▼

Over the years Australian slang has added a lot of colour to the English language. The following is a quick and easy reference.

⟩ ALCOHOLIC DELIGHTS ⟨

Amber fluid

Chateau de cardboard

Coldies

Darwin stubby

Deep sinker

Gee and tee

Grin and chronic

Heart-starter

Jimmy Woodser

Liquid amber

Liquid lunch

Lunatic soup

Plonk

Shearer's joy

Stubbies

Ten-ounce sandwich

Tinnies

ANGRY/FURIOUS

Berko

Bent as a scrub tick

Crooked on

Dark on

Dirty on

Mad as a cut snake

Mad as a gumtree

Maggoty

Ropeable

Toey

AUSTRALIA

Bazzaland

Down Under

Oz

AUSTRALIAN

All wool and a yard wide

Australian as a meat pie

Dinkum

Fair dinkum

True blue

BABY/CHILD

Ankle-biter

Billy/billy lid

Carpet grub

Kiddiewink

Little Vegemite

Nipper

Rug-rat

Whippersnapper

⟩ BLOWFLY ⟨

Butcher's canary

⟩ BROKE/PENNILESS ⟨

Hasn't got a bean

Hasn't got a brass razoo

Hasn't got a cracker

Stony broke

Stumped up

⟩ BROKEN ⟨

Buggered

Bung

Jiggered

On the blink

Onkus

Stuffed

Up the pole

Up the spout

CHAT

Bat the breeze

Chew the fat

Chinwag

Yabber

COUNTRY BUMPKIN/RUSTIC INDIVIDUAL

Bastard from the bush

Bushie/Bushwhacker

Dubbo

Geebung

DARING

Game as a piss-ant

Game as Ned Kelly

DEAD

Cactus

Clagged the bag

Dead as mutton chops

DEPRESSED

Happy as a bastard on Father's Day

Happy as a boxing kangaroo in a fog

Miserable as a bandicoot

DESPICABLE PERSON

Arsehole

Dingo

Dipstick

Low as shark shit

Lower than a snake's belly

Scumbag

Wouldn't piss on him if he was on fire

Wouldn't use him for sharkbait

DIFFICULT

Easy as pushing shit uphill with a toothpick

Easy as spearing an eel with a spoon

DRUNK/INTOXICATED

Away with the pixies/birdies

Blind

Dead to the world

Drunk as Chloe

Cut

Elephant's/Elephant's trunk

Flaked out

Full as a boot

Full as a fairy's phone book

Full as a fat woman's sock

Full as a goog

Full as a state school

Full as a tick

Lit up like a Manly ferry

Lit up like a Christmas tree

Loaded

Molly the monk

Out to it

Paralytic

Pissed as a newt

Pissed as a parrot

Pissed as a possum

Rotten as a chop

Shickered

Shot full of holes

Snakes hissed

Stonkered

Stunned

Tanked

Three parts gone

Three sheets to the wind

Tired and emotional

Under the affluence of inkahol

Under the weather

Well under

Zonked

ECCENTRIC PERSON

Dag

Dingbat

Poon

Ratbag

⟩ EGG ⟨

Cackleberry
Goog/Googy

⟩ EXCELLENT ⟨

Bee's knees
Beaut
Bobby-dazzler
Bonzer
Bosker
Bottler
Crash hot
Extra grouse
Pure merino
Ryebuck
Out of the box
Trimmer

⟩ EXHAUSTED ⟨

Buggered
Bushed
Clagged out
Tuckered out

EXTREMELY BUSY

Busy as a one-armed billposter in a gale

Flat out like a lizard drinking

Flat to the boards

Nose down, bum up

EXTREMELY COLD WEATHER

Brass monkey weather

Cold as a bushman's grave

Cold enough to freeze the medals off a brass monkey

EXTREMELY HUNGRY

Could eat a galah and bark sandwich

Could eat a goanna between two slabs of bark

Could eat a horse and chase the rider

Hungry as a black dog

My stomach thinks me throat's cut

EXTREMELY THIRSTY

Dry as a dead dingo's donger

Dry as a gum-digger's dog

Dry as a kookaburra in the Simpson Desert

Dry as a Pom's towel

FELLOW

Bleeder

Bloke

Coot

FIGHT/SCUFFLE

Barney

Blue

Rough-up

Run-in

FIGHTING FIT

Could kick the arse off an emu

Fit as a mallee bull

Fit as a mallee trout

FIRED (FROM JOB)

Got the arse/axe

Received the order of the boot

FLASHILY DRESSED

All laired up

Done up like a pet lizard

Done up like a pox-doctor's clerk

Flash as a rat with a gold tooth

Mockered up

Pooned up

FOODS

Cackleberry *(egg)*

Chook *(chicken)*

Cocky's joy *(golden syrup)*

Damper *(bushman's bread)*

Dead horse *(sauce)*

Dog's eye *(meat pie)*

Floater *(meat pie in a bowl of peas or gravy)*

Fly bog *(jam)*

Goog/Goggy-egg *(egg)*

Hen fruit *(egg)*

Johnny cake *(type of damper)*

Murphy *(potato)*

Mystery bags *(sausages)*

Sammie *(sandwich)*

Sanger *(sandwich)*

Sinker *(meat pie)*

Snag *(sausage)*

Underground mutton *(rabbit)*

HORSE

Alligator

Brumby

Crocodile

Moke

Prad

HOTEL/ROUGH PUBLIC HOUSE

Bloodhouse
Boozer
Lamb-down shop
Poison shop
Rubbity/rubbity dub

IDIOT

Beecham's Pill
Cough drop
Dill
Dingaling
Dingbat
Dingdong
Dipstick
Drongo
Droob
Dropkick
Galah
Gink
Mopoke
Ningnong
Wally

IN TROUBLE

In the cactus
In the poo on a sticky wicket

Up a gumtree

Up shit creek without a paddle

INEFFECTUAL/INCOMPETENT

Couldn't fart into a bottle

Couldn't fight his way out of a paper bag

Couldn't give away cheese at a rat's picnic

Couldn't knock the skin off a rice pudding

Couldn't last a round in a revolving door

Couldn't run a chook raffle in a country pub

Couldn't train a choko vine over a country dunny

Couldn't win if he started the night before

If he bought a kangaroo it wouldn't hop

Must have got his/her licence out of a Cornflakes packet

Only got one oar in the water

So wet you could shoot ducks off him

Weak as a wet whistle

Weak as cat's piss

INSANE/MENTALLY DERANGED

Around the twist

Barmy as a bandicoot

Bats

Bent as a scrub tick

Bonkers

Berko

Gone to Gowings

Has got some palings off the fence

Has got white ants in the woodwork

Kangaraoos in the top paddock

Mad as a cut snake

Mad as a gumtree full of galahs

Nits in the network

Off your kadoova

Have a go, ya mug!

Bite your bum!

Don't pick your nose or your head will cave in!

Go and take a running jump at yourself!

Go dip your eye in hot cocky cack

I wouldn't piss on him if he was on fire

I'll knock your teeth so far down your throat you'll have to stick a
toothbrush up your arse to clean them!

I've seen a better head on a glass of beer

Pull your head in!

Put a cork/sock in it!

What do you think this is – bush week?

What the bloody hell's crawlin' on you, mate?

You'd make a blowfly sick!

Bag of fruit *(suit)*

Bathers *(swimming costume)*

Cossie *(swimming costume)*

Cunnamulla cartwheel *(wide-brimmed hat)*

Daks *(trousers)*
Duds *(trousers)*
Egg-boiler *(bowler hat)*
Lunatic hat *(wide-brimmed hat)*
Monkey suit *(formal dinner suit)*
Thongs *(sandals with thong between big toe and next toe)*
Trunks *(swimming costume)*

KOOKABURRA

Breakfast bird
Bushman's clock
Ha-ha pigeon
Jackass
Settler's clock
Woop-Woop pigeon

LOOK

Captain Cook
Butcher's/Butcher's hook
Dekko
Gander
Geek

LONELY/OUT OF PLACE

All alone like a country dunny
Like a lily on a dustbin
Like a one-legged man at an arse-kicker's picnic

Like a pickpocket at a nudist camp
Like a shag on a rock
Lonely as a bandicoot on a burnt ridge
On your Pat Malone

LOUT

Bodgie

Bogan

Hoon

Larrikin

Mug lair

Yobbo

MONEY

Axlegrease

Big bickies

Dosh

Folding stuff

Quids

Smackers/smackeroos

NEW ZEALAND

Kiwiland

Land of the Long White Shroud

Quaky Isles

Beauty!

Bleeding oath!

Buggered if I know!

Drop off!

Fair crack of the whip!Fair go!

Fair suck of the sauce!

Good on ya!

Jesus wept!

Kiss my arse!

Nickywoop!

Not on your nelly!

Onya!

Pull your head in!

Put a cork/sock in it!

Put up your dooks!

Strewth!

Strike a light!

Too right!

Tough titty!

Turn it up!

Up there Cazaly!

You little beauty!

You der!

Wouldn't it rip you!

Wouldn't it rot your socks!

Wouldn't it root you!

OCCUPATIONS

Barber *(Sydney harbour)*

Bookmaker *(bookie)*

Boundary rider *(topwire lizard)*

Carpenter *(chippie)*

Cattle thief *(duffer/gullyraker)*

Cattle station worker *(jackaroo, jillaroo)*

Clergyman *(amen-snorter/bible-basher/god-botherer/sky pilot)*

Dairy farmer *(cow-cockie)*

Dentist *(fang-carpenter/gumpuncher)*

Dingo-hunter *(dog-stiffener)*

Doctor *(quack)*

Electrician *(sparkie)*

Farmer *(ground parrot/cockatoo/cockie)*

Land speculator *(land shark)*

Parking officer *(grey ghost)*

Plumber *(dunny diver)*

Police *(blues/boys in blue/ducks and geese/troopers/wallopers)*

Prostitute *(chromo/mallee root)*

Public servant *(shiny arse)*

Teacher *(chalkie)*

Tramp *(bagman/sundowner/swagman/swaggie)*

OLD PEOPLE

Crumblies

Old crackers

Oldies

PREGNANT

Bun in the oven

In the club

In the pudding club

Preggers

Up the duff

Up the spout

REMOTE AUSTRALIA

Back o' Bourke

Black Stump

Middle of nowhere

Outback

Where the crows fly backwards to keep the sun out of their eyes

Woop-Woop

SHARK

After dark

Noah/ Noah's ark

SHEEP

Jumbuck

SPORTING EXPRESSIONS

Have a go, ya mug!

Barrack for

Carn!

Chewie on ya boot!

Crumb-gatherer

Daisy-cutter

Howzat?

Up there Cazaly!

STATE INHABITANTS

New South Welshperson *(cornstalk)*

Northern Territorian *(top ender)*

Queenslander *(banana-bender)*

South Australian *(crow-eater/magpie/pie-eater)*

Tasmanian *(mutton bird/tassie tiger)*

Victorian *(cabbage-patcher)*

West Australian *(sandgroper)*

STUPID/SLOW-WITTED

Brick short of a load

Bright as a two-watt bulb

Couldn't run guts for a slow butcher

Few stubbies short of a six-pack

Going through life with the porch light on dim

Got space to sell between the ears

If his brains were dynamite he couldn't blow his hat off

Lights are on but there's nobody home

Not the full quid

Not the full two-bob

Only fifty cards in the pack
Sandwich short of a picnic
Short of numbers in the Upper House
Snag short of a barbecue
Thick as a brick
Thick as the dust on a public servant's out-tray
Three pots short of a shout
Tinny short of a six-pack
Wouldn't know his arse from his elbow

SYCOPHANT

Arse-licker
Crawler
Brown-noser

TIGHT-FISTED

Mean as bird-shit
Mean as Hungry Tyson
Mingy
So mean that when a fly lands in the sugar
he shakes it before he kills it
So mean he wouldn't give a rat a railway pie
Wouldn't give you the time of day
Wouldn't shout in a shark attack

TO DEPART

Arse off

Blow through
Choof off
Do a flit
Do a moonlight flit
Nick off
Off like a bride's nightie
Off like a bucket of prawns
Off like a robber's dog
Shot shrough like a Bondi tram
Skedaddle
Went through without the water bag

> TO DIE <

Cark it
Croak
Do a perish
Pass over the Great Divide
See your last gumtree
Snuff it

> TO IRRITATE YOU <

Get on your goat
Give you the irrits
Give you the Jimmy Brits
Give you the shits

> TO LOSE YOUR TEMPER <

Blow a fuse

Chuck a wobbly

Do your block/lolly/nana

Flip your lid

Get off your bike

Get your dander up

Go to market

> TO URINATE <

Drain the dragon

Point Percy at the porcelain

Splash the boots

Strain the potatoes

Syphon the python

Water the horses

> TO VOMIT <

Bark at the lawn

Call 'Ralph'

Chunder

Drive the porcelain bus

Park a tiger on the rug

Speak on the big white telephone

Spew

Technicolor yawn

Thrown (one's) voice

UNLUCKY PERSON

If he bought a kangaroo it wouldn't hop

If it was raining palaces he'd be hit on the head by a dunny door

If it was raining virgins he'd be locked in the dunny with a poofter

WIFE

Ball and chain

Trouble and strife

WILD PARTY

Bash

Booze-up

Rort

Shivoo

THE BASTARD FROM THE BUSH

▼ ▼ ▼

As night was falling slowly on city, town and bush
From a slum in Jones's Alley came the Captain of the Push,
And his whistles, loud and piercing, woke the echoes of the Rocks,
And a dozen ghouls came slouching round the corners of the blocks.

Then the Captain jerked a finger at a stranger by the kerb,
Whom he qualified politely with an adjective and verb.
Then he made the introduction: 'Here's a covey from the bush;
F— me blind, he wants to join us, be a member of the Push!'

Then the stranger made this answer to the Captain of the Push:
Why f— me dead, I'm Foreskin Fred, the Bastard from the Bush!
I've been in every two-up school from Darwin to the Loo;
I've ridden colts and brumbies; what more can a bugger do?'

'Are you game to break a window?' said the Captain of the Push.
'I'd knock a f—ing house down!' said the Bastard from the Bush.
'Would you out a man and rob him?' said the Captain of the Push.
'I'd knock him down and f— him!' said the Bastard from the Bush.

'Would you dong a bloody copper if you caught the c— alone?
Would you stoush a swell or Pommie, split his garret with a stone?
Would you have a moll to keep you; would you swear off work for good?'

Said the Bastard: 'My colonial silver-mounted oath – I would!'

'Would you care to have a gasper?' said the Captain of the Push.
'I'll take the bloody packet!' said the Bastard from the Bush.
Then the Pushites all took council, saying, 'F– me, but he's game!
Let's make him our star basher; he'll live up to his name.'

So they took him to their hideout, that Bastard from the Bush,
And granted him all privileges appertaining to the Push.
But soon they found his little ways were more than they could stand,
And finally their Captain addressed the members of his band:

'Now listen here, you buggers, we've caught a f–ing Tartar.
At every kind of bludging, that Bastard is a starter.
At poker and at two-up he's shook our f–ing rolls;
He swipes our f–ing likker and he robs our bloody molls!'

So down in Jones's Alley all the members of the Push
Laid a dark and dirty ambush for that Bastard from the Bush.
But against the wall of Riley's pub the Bastard made a stand,
A nasty grin upon his dial; a bike-chain in each hand.

They sprang upon him in a bunch, but one by one they fell,
With crack of bone, unearthly groan, and agonising yell,
Till the sorely battered Captain, spitting teeth and gouts of blood,
Held an ear all torn and bleeding in a hand bedaubed with mud.

'You low polluted Bastard!' snarled the Captain of the Push,
'Get back where your sort belongs – That's somewhere in the Bush.
And I hope heaps of misfortunes may soon tumble down on you;

May some lousy harlot dose you till your ballocks turn sky-blue!

May the itching piles torment you; may corns grow on your feet!
May crabs as big as spiders attack your balls a treat!
And when you're down and outed, to a hopeless bloody wreck,
May you slip back through your arsehole and break your f– ing neck!

Anon (attributed in part to Henry Lawson)

STIR THE WALLABY STEW

▼ ▼ ▼

Poor Daddy's got five years or more, as everynody knows;
And now he lives in Boggo Road, broad arrows on his clothes.
He branded all Brown's cleanskins, and never left a trail,
So I'll relate the family's fate, since Dad got put in jail.

Chorus: So stir the wallaby stew,
Make soup with the kangaroo's tail,
I tell you things are pretty crook
Since Dad got put in jail.

Our sheep all died a month ago, not rot, but flaming fluke.
Our cow was boozed last Christmas Day by my big brother Luke;
And Mother has a shearer cove forever within hail,
The family will have grown a bit when Dad gets out of jail.

Our Bess got shook upon a bloke, he's gone we don't know where.
He used to act around the sheds, but he ain't acted square.
I've sold the buggy on my own, the place is up for sale.
That isn't all that won't be junked when Dad gets out of jail.

They let Dad out before his time to give us a surprise.
He came and looked around the place, and gently damned our eyes.
He shook hands with the shearer cove, and said he thought things stale,
So he left him there to shepherd us, And battled back to jail.

Anon

DINKY DI

▼ ▼ ▼

He came over to London and straight away strode,
To army headquarters in Horseferry Road,
To see all the bludgers who dodge all the strafe,
By getting soft jobs on the headquarters staff.
Dinky di, dinky di,
By getting soft jobs on the headquarters staff.

A lousy lance-corporal said, 'Pardon me, please,
You've mud on your tunic and blood on your sleeve,
You look so disgraceful the people will laugh,'
Said the lousy lance-corporal on the headquarters staff.
Dinky di, dinky di,
Said the lousy lance-corporal on the headquarters staff.

The digger then shot him a murderous glance;
He said 'We're just back from the balls-up in France,
Where bullets are flying and comforts are few,
And brave men are dying for bastards like you;
Dinky di, dinky di,
And brave men are dying for bastards like you.'

'We're shelled on the left and we're shelled on the right,
We're bombed all the day and we're bombed all the night,
And if something don't happen, and that pretty soon,
There'll be nobody left in the bloody platoon;

Dinky di, dinky di,
There'll be nobody left in the bloody platoon.'

This story soon got to the ears of Lord Gort,
Who gave the whole matter a great deal of thought,
He awarded the digger a VC and bars,
For giving that corporal a kick up the arse;
Dinky di, dinky di,
For giving that corporal a kick up the arse.

Now when this war's over and we're out of here,
We'll see him in Sydney town begging for beer.
He'll ask for a dina to buy a small glass,
But all he'll get is a kick up the arse.
Dinky di, dinky di,
But all he'll get is a kick up the arse.

Anon

ALL FOR ME GROG

▼ ▼ ▼

Well I am a ramblin' lad, and me story it is sad,
If ever I get to Lachlan I should wonder,
For I spent all me brass in the bottom of the glass,
And across the western plains I must wander.

Chorus: And it's all for me grog, me jolly, jolly grog,
It's all for me beer and tobacco,
For I spent all me tin in a shanty drinking gin,
Now across the western plains I must wander.

Well I'm stiff, stony broke and I've parted from me moke,
And the sky is lookin' black as flamin' thunder;
The shanty boss is blue 'cause I haven't got a sou,
That's the way they treat you when you're down and under.

I'm crook in the head and I haven't been to bed,
Since first I touched this shanty with me plunder.
I see centipedes and snakes, and I'm full of aches and shakes,
And I think it's time to push for way out yonder.

I'll take to the Old Man Plain, and criss-cross him once again,
Until me eyes the track no longer see, boys;
And me beer and whisky brain search for sleep, but all in vain,
And I feel as if I've had the Darling Pea, boys.

So it's hang yer jolly grog, yer hocussed shanty grog,
    The beer that is loaded with tobacco;
Graftin' humour I am in, and I'll stick the peg right in
    And settle down once more to some hard yakka.

Anon

THE NEVER-NEVER LAND

▼ ▼ ▼

By homestead, hut, and shearing-shed,
By railroad, coach, and track –
By lonely graves where rest our dead,
Up Country and Out Back;
To where beneath the clustered stars
The dreamy plains expand –
My home lies wide a thousand miles
In the Never-Never Land.

It lies beyond the farming-belts,
Wide wastes of scrub and plain,
A blazing desert in the drought,
A lake-land after rain;
To the skyline sweeps the waving grass,
Or whirls the scorching sand –
A phantom land, a mystic realm!
The Never-Never Land.

Where lone Mount Desolation lies,
Mounts Dreadful and Despair,
'Tis lost beneath the rainless skies
In hopeless deserts there;
It spreads nor'– west by No-Man's Land –
Where clouds are seldom seen –

To where the cattle stations lie
Three hundred miles between.

The drovers of the Great Stock Routes
The strange Gulf Country know,
Where, travelling for the northern grass,
The big lean bullocks go;
And camped by night where plains lie wide
Like some old ocean's bed,
The stockmen in the starlight ride
Round fifteen hundred head.

And west of named and numbered days
The shearers walk and ride,
Jack Cornstalk and the Ne'er-do-well
And Greybeard side by side;
They veil their eyes from moon and stars,
And slumber on the sand –
Sad memories sleep as years go round
In Never-Never Land.

O rebels to society!
The Outcasts of the West –
O hopeless eyes that smile for me,
And broken hearts that jest!
The pluck to face a thousand miles –
The grit to see it through!
The communism perfected –
Till man to man is True

The Arab to the desert sand,
The Finn to fens and snow,
The 'Flax-stick' dreams of Maoriland,
While seasons come and go.
Whatever stars may glow or burn
O'er lands of East and West,
The wandering heart of man will turn
To one it loves the best.

Lest in the city I forget
True mateship, after all,
My waterbag and billy yet
Are hanging on the wall.
And I, to save my soul, again
Would tramp to sunsets grand
With sad-eyed mates across the plain
In the Never Never Land.

Henry Lawson

THE GEEBUNG POLO CLUB

▼ ▼ ▼

It was somewhere up the country, in a land of rock and scrub,
That they formed an institution called the Geebung Polo Club.
They were long and wiry natives from the rugged mountainside,
And the horse was never saddled that the Geebungs couldn't ride;
But their style of playing polo was irregular and rash —
They had mighty little science, but a mighty lot of dash:
And they played on mountain ponies that were muscular and strong
Though their coats were quite unpolished, and their manes and tails
were long.
And they used to train these ponies wheeling cattle in the scrub;
They were demons, were the members of the Geebung Polo Club.

It was somewhere down the country, in a city's smoky steam,
That a polo club existed, called the Cuff and Collar Team.
As a social institution, 'twas a marvellous success,
For the members were distinguished by exclusiveness and dress.
They had natty little ponies that were nice, and smooth, and sleek,
For their cultivated owners only rode 'em once a week.
So they started up the country in pursuit of sport and fame,
For they meant to show the Geebungs how they ought to play the game;
And they took their valets with them — just to give their boots a rub
Ere they started operations at the Geebung Polo Club.

Now my readers can imagine how the contest ebbed and flowed
When the Geebung boys got going it was time to clear the road;

And the game was so terrific that ere half the time was gone
A spectator's leg was broken – just from merely looking on.
For they waddied one another till the plain was strewn with dead,
While the scores were kept so even that they neither got ahead.
And the Cuff and Collar captain, when he tumbled off to die,
Was the last surviving player – so the game was called a tie.

By the old Campaspe River, where the breezes shake the grass,
There's a row of little gravestones that the stockmen never pass,
For they bear a crude inscription saying, 'Stranger, drop a tear,
For the Cuff and Collar players and the Geebung boys lie here.'
And on misty moonlit evenings, while the dingoes howl around,
You can see their shadows flitting down that phantom polo ground;
You can hear the loud collisions as the flying players meet,
And the rattle off the mallets, and the rush of ponies' feet,
Till the terrified spectator rides like blazes to the pub –
He's been haunted by the spectres of the Geebung Polo Club.

A.B. 'Banjo' Paterson

THE GREAT AUSTRALIAN SLANGUAGE

▼ ▼ ▼

'Tis the everyday Australian
Has a language of his own
Has a language, or a slanguage
Which can simply stand alone.
And 'a dicken pitch to kid us'
Is a synonym for 'lie',
And to 'nark it' means to stop it,
And to 'nit it' means to fly!

And bosom friend's a 'cobber',
And a horse a 'prad' or 'moke',
While a casual acquaintance
Is a 'joker' or a 'bloke',
And his lady-love's his 'donah',
Or his 'clinah' or his 'tart',
Or his 'little bit o' muslin',
As it used to be his 'bart'.

And his naming of the coinage
Is a mystery to some,
With his 'quid' and 'half-a'caser',
And his 'deener' and his 'scrum',
And a 'tin-back' is a party

Who's remarkable for luck,
And his food is called his 'tucker'
Or his 'panem' or his 'chuck'.

A policeman is a 'johnny',
Or a 'copman' or a 'trap',
And a thing obtained on credit
Is invariable a 'strap'.
A conviction's known as 'trouble',
And a gaol is called a 'jug',
And a sharper is a 'speiler',
And a simpleton's a 'tug',

If he hits a man in fighting
That is what he calls a 'plug',
If he borrows money from you,
He will say he 'bit your lug'.
And to 'strike it' is to beg;
And a jest is 'poking borac',
And a jester 'pulls your leg'.

Things are 'cronk' when they go wrongly
In the language of the 'push',
And when things go as he wants 'em
He declares it is 'all cush'
When he's bright he's got a 'napper'
And he's 'ratty' when he's daft,
And when looking for employment
He is 'out of blooming graft'.

And his clothes he calles his 'clobber'
Or his 'togs', but what of that
When a 'castor' or a 'kady'
is the name he gives his hat!
And our undiluted English
Is a fad to which we cling,
But the great Australian language
Is a truly awful thing!

W.T. Goodge

• ICONS •

> THE PAVLOVA

This fluffy, white meringue dessert was invented by Perth chef Bert Sachse to honour the great Russian ballerina Anna Pavlova.

Pavlova toured Australia in 1926 and 1929, performing in towns and cities across Australia. Her shows were so successful that her Melbourne season had to be extended three times.

Typical ingredients of the pavlova are egg whites, sugar, cornflour, vinegar, vanilla essence and cream of tartar, and a popular topping is chopped bananas, strawberries, kiwi fruit and of course, cream.

• ICONS •

THE BILLY

The billy is one of the most commonly used cooking implements Australians take with them on camping trips. Found in just about any camping store, the billy is ideal for making billy tea or heating up a quick meal of baked beans by the fire.

The billy is thought to have originated on the Victorian goldfields, the name coming from the Aboriginal word for creek or river – billabong. When one thinks of a billy, the image of the Aussie sitting on a log by the campfire making billy tea springs to mind, and that's why it's one of Australia's enduring icons.

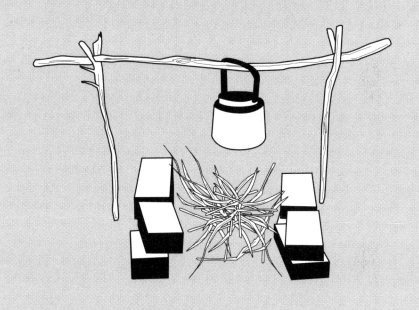